God Said, We Said

The Interpersonal Act of Creation

God Said, We Said

The Interpersonal Act of Creation

Robert E. Joyce

LifeCom

Published by
LifeCom
St. Cloud, Minnesota, USA

ISBN 978-0-9615722-9-7

For information, address *LifeCom*, Box 1832, St. Cloud, MN 56302

Contents

Preface

Sincere believers in God know and love the truth. But they make claims and draw conclusions that beg for better explanations. This book is written to offer deeper meaning to believers and to those who are earnestly seeking God, who is worshipped and celebrated by Jews, Christians, and Muslims.

People who acknowledge the one personal God are called theists. They are the spiritual children of Abraham, brothers and sisters in a common divine communication intended for all people. As a theist, I praise and thank God for the divine Revelation. I hope to advance our ability to *receive* this Revelation. My basic purpose is to provide deeper premises and perspectives so that we will be better able to receive.

I have tried to avoid concepts and terms that are technical, so that the book is accessible to most people who are keenly attracted to the mystery of creation and the origin of evil. But if the reader thinks that some passages of the book are difficult to understand, such can be skipped without missing the fundamental message of the new theistic perspective.

Also, subsequent works are planned for those who would desire even more concentrated developments of the new view.

In any event, I am profoundly indebted to the basic teachings of the Catholic Church, to which I am committed for life. My hope is that the new viewpoints for receiving Revelation might serve to amplify and enrich the meaning of those teachings. Some Catholic doctrines are common, and some are unique, within the three main traditions of theism. Despite any impressions to the contrary, I think that nothing held in this book of exploration opposes the teaching authority of the Church.

Discordant notes are sounded, however, concerning the present state of *theological* development. Theology includes the endeavor of explaining the truths received in Scripture, Tradition, and Nature— and harmonizing them.

The book's anecdotes and examples have varying characteristics. All are based on real happenings. Some are fictionalized, at least partly, either to protect the parties involved or to bring some points to a finer pitch. Some serve more as parables than as reports.

For review and helpful comments on certain aspects of Jewish and Islamic teaching, I am grateful to Professor Seth Ward, currently teaching at the University of Wyoming. At the time, he was Director of the Institute for Islamic-Judaic Studies, located at the University of Denver. His review occurred in the early stages of writing and he cannot be faulted for any inadequacies in the final rendition.

Thanks to all those who read the manuscript in various stages of development. Readers of the whole book include three people who deserve particular mention.

James T. Joyce, my brother, is a writer who afforded immediate encouragement and suggested developments for the overall work.

The late Dorothy T. Samuel, friend and author with penetrating faith, gave valuable help both on the content and the presentation.

Mary Rosera Joyce, my best friend, beloved spouse, and fellow philosopher, has been involved with every phase of this work. She and I have discussed all of the major points and so many secondary ones that she could have written the book herself. In such case, she would have provided her own distinctive angles with a very similar message.

Thanks are due to Mary particularly for ideas and phrases such as passive-reactive energy, the need to anchor the beginning of the book in *Genesis*, the idea of renewal in the roots, and the concept of humans being rational persons—and not animals in anything but a figurative sense.

Mary and I have been married in life and in thought since 1961. I deeply cherish her loving work with this book and the others I have published.

The ideas for the present endeavor have been gestating since 1964. The key insight came to me suddenly in the midst of an informal discussion with a small group of University faculty members who were concerned with creation and evolution.

This book is basically an introduction to the development and to the deepening of the meaning of creation, sin, and redemption. On behalf of the added work that is forthcoming, I welcome readers' questions, suggestions, comments, and critique.

Robert E. Joyce, Ph.D.
Professor Emeritus
St. John's University
Collegeville, Minnesota
January 1, 2010

LifeCom
Box 1832
St. Cloud, MN 56302

Email: robertjoyce@charter.net
Website: www.lifemeaning.com

Introduction

If this God is omnipotent, he could have prevented the Holocaust. If he was unable to stop it, he is impotent and useless; if he could have stopped it and chose not to, he is a monster. Jews are not the only people who believe that the Holocaust put an end to conventional theology (376).

Karen Armstrong
A History of God

Armstrong challenges the future of belief in God. She and millions of others deserve an effective response. But what can be reasonably said?

From the traditional point of view, as systematically developed so far, how can any reply be convincing?

The standard theologies of the God-worshipping cultures seem to be trapped by their own logic. They attend to these questions: *Why* is there evil in the world and *why* does God allow innocent persons to suffer? Yet they characteristically relegate these wonderings of the soul to being inaccessible, consummate mysteries.

God is said to be *infinitely loving*. But God is also assumed to be unwilling or even unable to prevent grave injustice from coming to created persons who seem obviously not responsible for it. Serious reflection then inevitably asks *why such creatures* are allowed to exist under conditions that are not deserved in the first place. Why could not these innocent ones have been created and "placed" in a different kind of world?

Many have often opined that God will compensate these unduly afflicted persons for their sufferings. Perhaps, in the next world, they will be given an unimaginably grand reward.

But this claim begs the question. Why must they endure *any* evil, *if they are free of any personal fault and if God's love for them is truly unlimited?*

Issues like these raise the specter of the apparent "impotence of God." Often they have been considered too hot to handle. Or they have been virtually repressed. From the *Book of Job* unto the latest speculations, the main *why* questions receive attention that is, at best, indirect.

Historically, the approach of religious writing on evil and on pain seems to be an attempt to ease our symptoms, without encountering directly and systematically the mystery of their origins.

In relatively recent times, authors of various kinds articulate well the problem of pain and misery. From Dostoyevsky to Dobson, many provide solutions that are valuable in themselves. But their efforts may also amount to suggesting ways to find comfort for the sufferers *without* gaining an understanding of the *chief cause* of *all* affliction and heartache. These authors are inclined to slip away from the questions of *why* and *how* there can be any suffering at all *for the innocent.*

There are exceptions to this tendency to slide into comforting the afflicted without finding the ultimate reason for the affliction. As an individual sufferer and counselor of many, Rabbi Pesach Krauss discovered ever-deeper meaning for our trials. And he even reached into the deep wisdom of Rabbi Levi Yitzchak of Berditchev for his remarkable prayer. Rabbi Yitzchak prays, "Merciful Father…I don't question your righteous rule. I just want you to reveal to me why I suffer, that I can carry whatever burdens you place upon me and endure any test with which you confront me" (110).

Like Viktor Frankl and others, Rabbi Krauss knows that we can endure any amount of suffering if we have sufficient meaning. And he makes a breakthrough in his own life when he sees in suffering and death what he calls "an experience of growth and transition and transformation" (110). He still does not come to the basic answer to the question, *Why me?* But, unlike so many in the theistic tradition, the Rabbi seems to remain faithful to the truth that God's very being is *both* infinitely good *and* infinitely powerful. He finds a meaning for suffering that expands, even as he wrestles with the incredibly painful questions.

We all are inclined to ask, consciously or unconsciously, why did God allow presumably innocent children to suffer—or to be at risk to suffer—the most horrifying accidents, diseases, and deaths? Why not give each person a *fresh* start? Why not create another world that is as original as the presumed beginning for Adam and Eve? Why is each one of us bombed with the sin of our first parents? Why were we not given the opportunity *freely* to concur with that sin—or *freely* to reject it?

Original Victims

Typically, we are inclined to blame others for our own misdeeds, miscues, and negligence. But refusing responsibility for acting the way we do reaches the extreme when we go back to Adam and Eve as the first culprits. We are taught, in effect, to blame them *entirely* for the *origin* of evil in our world. We are given the impression that we are basically their victims.

Our daily excuses are fed by our thinking that, as we entered this world, our victimhood began. Unconsciously, we then blame God for creating us as progeny of Adam and Eve, rather than of some sinless couple in a different world.

In order to rationalize our victimization, grand attempts have been made. Christian theologians have undergone painful contortions of thought trying to explain how we could inherit the "sin of Adam" *without ourselves being personally* sinful. Original sin is even seen as personal in fact, without being our personal act.

In the Christian tradition, at least, our origin from Adam and Eve included *personal loss*: a kind of factual deprivation suffered by us *personally*. We descendants of Adam and Eve inherited a condition of sin that amounts to a deficit in our nature, contracted by human generation. We are the victims of our inherited nature as transmitted in space and time.

According to a common, unexamined assumption, God was *forced* to create us as children of Adam and Eve. We could not have had other first parents, who did not sin. Yet such an assumption betrays our willingness to overlook other truths. We pass over the *infinite* freedom, power, and goodness of God. And so we project onto God some of *our* ways of being and doing.

The theory of *why* we inherited the original sin was developed simplistically. It seems to be derived from within the necessarily closed psychology and sociopolitical framework of humankind, *as already devastated by sin*. The theory keeps us inside the box of temporal sequence. We fail to take seriously the *non*-temporal and *non*-spatial dimensions of God's activity in creating us. We become satisfied with an "outside story" of creation and sin.

In the world of space and time, of course, children inherit the bad the good from their parents. Accordingly, they are not considered responsible for any of it—the good or the bad. But, then, theologians and others extrapolate from this "after-the-fact" situation of parents imposing upon their progeny. Theorists regard the relationship of parents to children in this sinful world as though it has significant applicability to the way God treats us at the *very origin* of our *being*.

Today we can witness an extreme example of such projection, whereby our human ways of acting are attributed to God's ways.

Recently some theologians have stoked a "theology of protest." In the wake of the Holocaust, particular religious thinkers—especially Elie Wiesel, David Blumenthal, and others—are ready to accuse God of being an abusive parent. Blumenthal, at least, does so quite dramatically in his book, *Facing the Abusing God: A Theology of Protest*.

All theistic cultures instinctively attribute to God characteristics that could be only human. The anthropomorphic and anthropopathic literature found in the Hebrew Testament seems to lend itself to such *interpretations*—however inadequate these renderings might be.

In its fixation on the human predicament, the "protest theology" idea seems to hold that good psychology is good theology; and that bad psychology is bad theology. The emotional is privileged over the religious. So, the loss of a truly transcendent subject for theology continues, and even God is "put on the couch." When reflective people lack understanding of *being* (ontology), both theology and psychology suffer gravely.

Still, the rising attention to "protest thought" poignantly exhibits our perennial, unconscious hunger for the meaning of *being* that would support deeper ideas of God and of the human heart.

Even thinkers steeped in theistic tradition seem to be locked into the conscious or unconscious assumption that the first moment of our *being* had to be temporal and had to have temporal features. So, we are then forced to assume that God's will is "tied." God *could not have created us in any other way* than as subject to the "sin of Adam" in some sort of space and time.

Nevertheless, by this traditional theological version, the meaning of God's unlimited freedom to create *out of nothing* is "limited," apparently without the theorizers realizing it.

Losing Faith in God

Religious culture is suffering from a block and a lock. Our vision is blocked by the assumption that God's ways must be similar to our ways—even our spatial and temporal ways. And we are locked into this assumption by a fear that is *unconscious*. We "know" that, if we release ourselves from the space-time perspective, we will have to take far more responsibility for who we are, and for where we are, than we have done traditionally.

Unconsciously, we recoil instinctively from the idea that we might *not* be victims from the start. So, we cling to our victimhood. And we do not even recognize that we are doing so.

Regarding the meaning of evil at least, theism generally presents an escapist theology. The beginning of evil in innocent persons is avoided by calling it a "mystery."

Yet, for our finite and defective minds, *everything* natural as well as supernatural is a mystery. We can start with the simplest natural mysteries, such as gravity, electricity, and molecular differentiation. And we can wend our way into deeper mysteries.

Reason and faith work together to identify mysteries and to know more about them. The faith might be "natural faith" or "supernatural faith." But reason works within it for better or for worse.

Mysteries are really truths that are ever more knowable. They are not problems that block the mind and heart. Mysteries challenge us to know even more. And the more we "know into them"—the more we participate in them—the more we know how little we know. But we still know *more* than before.

When we enter upon "the mystery of the origin of evil" we are confronting a matter of Faith. But we are also looking for sufficient support in reason. We search for understanding that is ever more adequate, though never comprehensive. The truths of Faith call for healthy reasoning so that we can better articulate them to ourselves and to others.

But there seems to be a perennial block on how our *susceptibility* to evil originated. For instance, we even take the story of *Genesis* and read it as having a largely external impact, as though we were not *personally* involved in what it portrays.

The recent movement called the "theology of protest" is, in any case, facing traditional believers with their own logic—lodged in the minds of theists generally. The logic of the spatiotemporal lockdown signifies that everything God is doing *in relation to us* is to be given, consciously or unconsciously, a temporal framework that is perhaps also spatial. Because of this fixation, exercising "reason and Faith" can turn the hearts of many believers against divine Providence. At least, that has been done so overtly in the movement of protest.

In this theology of dissent, people devastated by the Holocaust are recognized as "certainly innocent" of its sins and crimes. God is then called upon to *repent to us* for gravely abusing his people. According to this perspective, we adults may have to repent for our own sins, but *God* has overreached in punishment. God is addressed like this: "…You were the Abuser; our sins were not commensurate with Your actions. The responsibility is Yours, not ours. You must ask forbearance from us, not we ask forgiveness from You. You must return to us, not we come back to You" (Blumenthal, 299).

For ages, we have been told that God alone is totally responsible for the actual existence of the cosmic world. But many questions are left unanswered concerning the meaning of this corruptible world, and especially concerning its toll in human suffering and planetary entropy. Is God infinitely good, but not infinitely powerful? Should not God be held personally responsible for the original defects of spatial and temporal existence? The lack of credible answers serves progressively to undermine the Judeo-Christian Faith.

In the "theology of protest," there is the manifest, prayerful, frank declaration that God is singularly responsible for considerable pain and suffering in the world. This stance should chasten believers. We are being called to realize that faith in God, as *infinitely* good and *infinitely* powerful, remains in a condition of conscious crisis. Ever emerging from the unconscious depths of the human predicament is the conflict between God's glory and our story.

Looking for the origin of *human* evil simply in this world of space and time and of the events in Eden constitutes a cosmic lockdown. It makes impossible even a preliminary resolution of the question *why innocents suffer*. For the support of Faith, we must look to a better philosophy of *being*. As Einstein is reported to have said, thinking of matters in science and creativity, 'a problem can never be solved at the same level of consciousness in which it arose.' All the more so, in matters of the mysteries of religion and personal destiny.

Right within the contents of Revelation, a more intimate, freer way to understand what we believe must be found. Otherwise, renewal of Faith by regeneration cannot flourish. The heart has its intuitions that, as yet, reason is disinclined to investigate.

Crisis in Receiving the Revelation

The vacuum in the theistic worldview allows New Age ideologies to flourish. Newly-minted Gnostic exercises exploit the stagnation in theistic meanings for creation, freedom, and sin. Besides, New Age thinkers are quite disinclined even to recognize the existence of an original evil that is *personal*—much less a God who is *personal*.

Such omissions serve as part of their present appeal. There is no ultimate personal responsibility for what has been called *sin*. The rapidly vanishing sense of wrongdoing is unhappily fueled by the incapacity of theists, who are unable to explain sufficiently the truly personal and individual origin of good and evil.

Within theism itself, we can hardly continue to offer inadequate explanations of evil. It does not suffice to say simply that God draws good out of evil. That claim is true. But the explanations about why and how the evil got there in the first place seem to be overlooking the elephant in the parlor. A post-holocaust faith is going to have to challenge *itself* as well as its detractors.

Books such as *Night* by Elie Wiesel, *A History of God* by Karen Armstrong, *How to Know God* by Deepak Chopra, and *When Bad Things Happen to Good People* by Harold Kushner, among many others, offer resistance to the Judeo-Christian-Islamic worldview. The keen interest evoked by these challenging books should put theists on notice. The traditional meaning for God and creation must truly deepen, or else millions more will drift away.

The slippage of believers seems largely prompted by an unfulfilled hunger for richer, more personal *meaning* in the areas of creation, sin, and redemption. Even the most edifying of traditional writings tend to block fulfillment of the need for extending and expanding the *roots* of theistic meaning.

Contemporary literary works act similarly. When dealing with the absolute origin of evil and the suffering of the innocent, they stray from the question *why*. Poet Les Murray writes of what he calls the "knockout question": Why does God not spare the innocent? And Murray claims that if people knew he (the writer) could answer it they would shrink in terror.

Some authors even bargain away the traditional meaning for God as being *both* infinitely good *and* infinitely powerful. The popular commentary, *When Bad Things Happen to Good People*, is but one prominent example. Multitudes of contemporary readers are being swayed into abandoning crucial dimensions of their faith, such as belief that God's power is truly *infinite*.

There are inadequately answered questions surrounding the all-good creation and the beginning of evil. Deeply felt quandaries have been rumbling over and under the surface for centuries. Today they seem to be shaking the ground of theistic belief.

Many seem to sense that something big is missing. Vast gaps can be recognized in the traditional interpretations of Scripture and in the progress of theology.

On the one hand, there are multitudes of perceptive worshippers. They appreciate movement forward, but their beliefs and practices beg for deeper religious meaning. They insist on keeping faith with the already mammoth tree of traditional theistic truth. And they are willing to let its roots grow deeper.

On the other hand, there are vast numbers who simply abandon the tree of traditional Revelation. They proceed to meander elsewhere. Many seem to be inclined to sink their feeble individual roots into the shifting sands of self-indulgent meaning. Revelation made by the living transcendent God, the *Holy* Other, is forsaken.

But the blockage persists. For example, the typical, dramatic face-off today between "creationism" and "evolutionism" constitutes part of the block. On the one side, Biblical literalists insist on making the Bible a kind of two-dimensional book of instruction. And they do not allow sufficient room for the profound dimension of ontological meaning that empowers the texts. On the other side, there are the theistic evolutionists who likewise trivialize latent meanings. They assume that God could create something directly *ex nihilo* ("out of nothing") by way of a *process*.

Both creationists and theistic evolutionists are somehow blocked from treating God as an immediate Gifter from the Heart—Person to person. They regard the Creator as the supreme Processor—whether the process lasts for six days or six aeons. They assume that they are speaking about creation *ex nihilo* ("out of nothing"). But they are dealing mainly with creation *ex aliquo* (out of *something*). Neither literalistic creationists nor theistic evolutionists appreciate, seriously enough, God creating us *out of nothing* in a manner that is Heart-to-heart, immediately and perfectly.

Notably, both parties confuse the two different kinds of divine creation. In the first kind of creation, God's infinite activity of Love causes the non-durational, pure *effects* of the act of creation. In the second, God responds compassionately—in the face of the partly-affirming, partly-negative response of many created persons to the first creation—by *causing* the remedial, cosmic universe and the *process* of its temporal effects.

These two kinds of creation—out of nothing (*ex nihilo*) and out of something (*ex aliquo*)—have not been carefully distinguished. Both creationists and theistic evolutionists fail to consider deeply enough not only *why* evil originated *personally*, but also *how*. And many do not see that, while every process is an activity, not every activity is a process.

As the old saying has it, "metaphysics buries its morticians." No one can escape the ontological principles and assumptions in any endeavor of knowledge. In fact, the debate between evolution and creationism could not possibly be adequately resolved by physical evidence alone. Such evidence would still require interpretations that are inevitably ontological, that is, based on the *being* of it all, not simply on the *becoming* or coming-to-be.

Both evolutionists and "creationists" overlook the primal origin of human *persons*. They seem to assume that the *absolute* beginning of these persons occurred on the planet earth or somewhere in space and time. But the origin of the human inhabitants of the physical universe—and the origin of the universe itself—is far from being the same as the absolute beginning of these persons: their creation "out of nothing." Evolutionists and their creationistic antagonists come weighted with principles that beg ontological examination.

So, there appears to be a critical need to exhume and discuss some of the ultimate principles taken for granted by believers in God who is truly transcendent—a Person and not a Process.

Other questions, too, must be addressed. These might lead toward answers to the *why and the how*.

Unanswered Questions

God's creative activity admits of genuine differences between the temporal and non-temporal dimensions of being, of reality. We can see that *Genesis* gives an account of creation that seems specifically temporal. If this account is really the whole creation story, where, for instance, is the non-temporal creation of the angels? In other words, where is God's *immediate* creation of persons *as persons*?

Is the *first* creative act so impersonal that God actually produces and works with a void? (*Genesis*: 1:2) Or, granted the originatively creative act was indeed *inter*personal, how could we merely *human* persons respond personally—as we immediately came to *be*?

The Bible asserts little about the interpersonal, *direct* response of the angels to God *at the moment of their creation*. Nor is there any indication about an *immediate* response from humans. We have only the idea that the first humans were made out of the dust of the earth and from a rib. Even under such conditions of process, did Adam say anything? Perhaps, he would say something like, "Thank you for creating me. Praise you, Father, for bringing me up out of the dust of the earth!"

In *Genesis*, Adam's *immediate* response to God's creating him is not even slightly suggested.

What we hear instead is God having Adam realize his loneliness, not having a companion like himself. He is permitted to name the animals. But if God's *act* of creation is perfect, why is Adam, the effect, imperfect? Why is he lonely? Why is he not complete?

Then, after making a companion for him, God listens to Adam talk about the woman as truly one with him. This man calls her "bone of my bones, flesh of my flesh."

God had already spoken with Adam and—implicitly at least—with Eve. They were given a special prohibition. They were told not to eat of the tree of the knowledge of good and evil. This tree was already "in their face," right in the middle of the Garden. If this "paradise" was perfect, why was anything even slightly connected with evil there *in the beginning*?

Other questions abound. How could God command Adam and Eve to increase and fill the earth by starting with incest between their children? Was there no generative sex activity in Eden because there was no death? If Adam and Eve had not sinned, and no offspring ever died, how would any of the billions or trillions of their progeny enter an ecstatic union with God? If Adam and Eve had not sinned, but some of their children did and others did not, how would "the world" be structured? If Eve sinned and Adam did not, or vice versa, what would *we* be like?

Genesis portrays reality. But much of the revelation's wording is symbolic of the still more profound dimension of *being*. Religious traditions interpret the essentials and teach authoritatively. But they convey only *the basics* about the creation, the temptation, and the consequences of the fall. Much deeper meaning for the Revelation might be attained. *Growth in the roots of the meaning* is crucial.

An Inside Story

The questions already mentioned and many others call for a deeper perspective. Faith necessarily involves the inherent cooperation of reason. The illuminations of Faith shine on *and through* the insights afforded by an informed and reflective experience. Common sense, science, history, theological anthropology, and even cosmological theories of being are not enough. We can face questions of origin and destiny only by understanding them *also* through an ontological viewpoint, that is, through what it means to *be*.

This reality-bearing standpoint requires an effort to observe things at a more integrative level. Among the features of both natural and supernatural *being,* we are called to determine their harmony. If we attain deeper meaning for ultimate realities, we can thereby become at least somewhat freer *right within* our inevitable conditioning by culture and society.

Suppose we deliberately seek the common ground of all reality—natural and supernatural. In general, the result would be a greater understanding of *being* as it *is* in itself. This explicitly *ontological*—not cryptically cosmological—philosophy would work *within* the theology of creation, freedom, and sin by enhancing it. An inside dimension of the creation story would be brought into view.

Many people perceive that the story of origins is more than what theological traditions have unfolded so far. Many others, however, are abandoning theism for Eastern pantheism. Yet, the minds of these wanderers continue to be blocked and locked. They search for a *deeper, ever-elusive* self. They become mired primarily in stories and philosophies that amount to being quite impersonal, lacking a primal dialogic "partner" who is divine.

Such seekers seem to be elevating their "self esteem" to the level of "the Self." Yet, in so doing, they identify their own finite being with the "infinite" Being of an *impersonal* kind of intelligence. *How to Know God* by Deepak Chopra skillfully delineates this approach. God is Process. The result is that "salvation" (*growth*) amounts to the seekers' own doing. Enlightenment becomes chiefly self-effort and not primarily the act of an infinitely intimate, *personal* God.

God Said, We Said attempts to convey an inside story of theistic creation. It is *an* inside story, not necessarily *the* inside story. The account tells of *interpersonal* activity. The narrative is non-Gnostic and straightforward. It is not the usual kind of story. But it describes something of the elementary structure and dynamics of *being* itself.

The description of creation "out of nothing" *and our response* requires the use of terms laden with the burden of space and time. But God's super-dynamic act of creating had no duration at all. Nor was it preceded by duration. It was an "immediate moment."

In the interest of vision, this ontological account or inside story is offered without burdening the reader with the *details* in logic and in theory of knowledge. We can come to see, perhaps for the first time, what it means for us to *be*. We attempt to realize how we are created "out of nothing" *and also* are free *immediately* to respond to the gift of our being.

This story behind the story of *Genesis* attempts to communicate, in at least some basic respects, our dignity emanating from the heart of God. We are given to know *why* even the most "innocent" of us are involved in the *origins* of both good and evil.

*****

A Word about Thinking

We will be thinking about the most profound depths of reality. This endeavor requires the exercise of a mind that is active in a wise manner, respectful of common sense and scientific reasoning, yet actively engaged within and beyond them. In order to attain the *uncommon* sense known as wisdom, we must get in touch with our ability to see things whole and against the wide sky of *being*.

Because the key ideas of this book are relatively new, they are presented repeatedly from various angles. The approach required is a global, more-than-linear one. The reader who is conscientious might thereby benefit from meditating on the new perspective in ways that could engender a deepening of personal worldview.

The self-centered, matter-bound perspectives found in pragmatic consciousness must be held in abeyance. We are looking fully into meanings that are paradoxical, involving the union of opposites.

The common logic of identity and separation, so necessary in both speculative and practical matters, will be needed, but can hardly be sufficient. Much of the truth in faith and philosophy is not like the *either-or truth* found in mathematics (e.g., "6 x 7 = 42, not 41.8," and so forth) and in practical matters (e.g., "this candidate will either win or lose the election").

By contrast, the truth of *being* permeates everything and is super-relational. Relating to everything, *being* is analogical, not univocal or *merely* logical. More than anything, the truth of *being* is a *both-and* kind of truth. It is inclusive of all lesser kinds of truth.

So, when we are thinking about *God, life*, our *origins*, and our *destiny*, one single meaning does not "fit all." The same word can have significantly different meanings. Depending on the context, as well as the worldview, the terms we use shift in meaning.

In ordinary conversation and writing, we are strongly prone to think about matters of simple practicality—where words can have meanings with only one or two dimensions. Such words necessarily have *univocal* and *separable* meanings. These everyday words have the *same* basic meaning each time they are used. One and the same word is said of diverse things with essentially the same meaning. Words like "dog" and "house" most often mean the same each time they are used.

So, when we enter philosophical and theological matters, we are not as inclined to think in terms of *both-and* meanings, wherein the same word can have quite different, yet related, meanings on various occasions. The mysteries of reality and of our limited minds require agile adjustments.

Theists, therefore, are called to do paradoxical (both-and) thinking about the greatest revelations of God. For instance, we acknowledge *both* the withinness *and* the otherness of God. The divine Being is known to be fully *within* creatures, as well as completely *other than* creatures. This immanence and transcendence of God is then a truth of an incomparable integration of opposites: God's *withinness* (not insideness) is integrated with God's *otherness* (*not* outsideness or "beyondness").

Theists profess that God is *both* infinitely "close to" *and also* infinitely other than created beings. Theists are neither pantheists, who think that creatures are ultimately identical to God—or form a part of God—nor deists, who think of creatures as separate from God. Theists *distinguish* clearly—*without separating*—uncreated Being and created being.

Failures of human understanding can be massive and often quite "complementary." For everyone who claims that "the sun is God" or that God is "in the starry heavens" there are many who think that God is the same as themselves or that they are part of God.

But theists hold that God is not separate from us, like a physical and spatial entity, nor identical to us, even in part, however much we "look inside." Fixated areas of the mind, impeding a true awareness of God, have to be relaxed and awakened by paradoxical thinking. Truth is *both* either-or *and* both-and; not *either* either-or *or* both-and.

There are truths that are either-or (such as, "you will be either saved or lost forever"); and there are truths that are both-and (such as, "God both can and cannot save you," depending on how well you exercise your personal freedom). While retaining respect for *either-or* truths, we must tap into the *both-and roots* of truth in order to grow in vigorous understanding.

God Said, We Said requires the kind of paradoxical thinking that sees truth unfolding from the unity of opposites. The transcendence and immanence of God is but one prime example of many such truths.

This book includes other paradoxical truths. Particularly relevant in light of the new theistic view is the meaning of being and of becoming. Creation *ex nihilo* (out of nothing), the creation of our *being*, has been constantly confused with creation *ex aliquo* (out of something; dust, a rib), the creation of our *becoming*. The book calls attention to our "cosmolock," our minds' lockage onto the world of matter and motion (cosmos). It points out how we tend to reduce *being* to *becoming* in one way or another, instead of giving respect to the two different terms. *Becoming* is a kind of *being.* But not every *being* entails *becoming.* God, for instance, does not become anything by growth or transition of any kind. Only by infinite love.

Important words in our everyday life—terms such as self, gift, causality, soul, and so many others—can have either being-based meaning or becoming-based meaning. It is helpful to see how these diverse meanings interface.

So, we need to refrain from an exclusive *either-or* mentality about our deepest kind of identity. Perennially, we are short-circuiting God's love for us by leaving out the *true* infinity of God and the *perfection* of originative creation (*ex nihilo*). We take finite persons as found in the cosmic, imperfect world and "forget" they were, and still are, *perfect* as effects of creation *ex nihilo.* Created human persons are *both* perfect *and* imperfect, not simplistically imperfect. That is a paradox second to none.

In any event, when we are trying to understand the new view, with many different angles and levels of meaning for common terms, it would be wise to hold back our tendencies to make univocal and simplistic judgments. By such restraint, unnecessary disagreements can be minimized, while genuine disagreements can become better focused.

All the while, we can hope for agreements—*both* old *and* new.

Chapter 1

The Shock of a Lifetime

Late for work, Alan backed his car out of the driveway. He heard a gentle thump. It seemed that he had run over something. He said to himself, "What did those kids leave in the driveway now?"

As the car moved into the street Alan saw, in a burst of horror, his toddler-son, Johnny. The child was limp on the driveway. He had died immediately. The sight of the tender remains will haunt this father for the rest of his life.

Soon after the accident, Alan and his wife, Stephanie, were angry with themselves and with each other. For a while, they even raged at God. They finally settled blame for Johnny's death on their own negligence. The manner of death, however, at the hand of the child's father, smolders in their hearts. They still wonder how God could have let this cruel twist of "providence" happen to them and to their son.

For many months after the tragedy, the pain was almost too much to bear. The three older children needed counseling. Both Alan and Stephanie entered into individual therapy and family counseling. They even separated for a while.

Now their marriage is stronger. Moreover, as part of their mission in life, they have become leaders in a group that helps other couples with troubled marriages.

Our Shock

In the awesome affliction suffered by this couple and their little boy, you and I are involved. We realize that something like this could happen to us. If it did, we too might cry out, "Why is this *happening* to me? What did I do to deserve something so bad? How could God *let* it happen?"

Every member of the human family on earth lives in the same predicament—on the verge of crashing into something and of being crushed. Most people have family or friends who have experienced disasters. And throughout the world poverty, homelessness, disease, and starvation devastate multitudes.

You do not have to be a Buddha to understand that life is painful. To live is to suffer, for yourself and for your fellow human beings. As the title of one book puts it, "If God is so good, why do I hurt so bad?" (Biebel)

Many folks, however, abide in relative luxury, free from serious illness and misfortune. Are they better persons, who deserve what they have? Some people seem to profit from their own wicked deeds. In addition, perhaps worst of all, many ordinary individuals live for themselves, prospering in spite of their indifference toward the plight of others. They show little concern for life's ultimate meaning. Why, then, must you and I suffer in body and mind, while others do not?

But, of course, they do. They are living in constant anxiety about losing their possessions, their health, and even life? Consciously or unconsciously, they suffer the prospects of a devastating disease or a severely impairing accident. The very world we live in—the whole of the space-time cosmos—is so structured that every day we walk on a tightrope, strung over a canyon of miseries. Yes, and in the end, at death, we are going to experience the loss of all the health and happiness that this precarious life can offer.

Right now, you might think life is an exciting challenge. You might feel ready to engage in this awesome adventure, no matter how it turns out. Nevertheless, you still know that this life will end in your absolute failure to function at all.

You and I are destined to die. We can die well or poorly; but we will not live and thrive for much more than 90 years. Not only the human individual, but also humankind itself can be seen to be only a microscopic blip in cosmic duration.

The physical universe is good and beautiful, but fatally flawed. If we are honest, we will let ourselves be vulnerable to the underlying truth that this world is steeped in the most amazing varieties and intensities of evil. We are living in a cosmic concentration camp. And no one gets out alive.

Who Is Responsible?

When bad things happen—whether to "good" people or "bad" people—who is the decisive cause of the evil in these happenings? Some pretend not to care. But most take life and death seriously. And many blame God for their pain.

Frank was a member of a Christian congregation. One frightening night the church was destroyed by arsonists. Some people, meeting in a basement room, were killed; others were severely burned. As he left the Church and his faith, he declared, "Maybe God is infinitely powerful, but not infinitely good. God might be a kind of 'sadist in the sky'—or at least He might have a bit of sadism on the side— while creating 'goodness and justice for all.' Surely an all-powerful Parent who fully loves a child would not allow bully parents on earth to injure this child."

But Doris, a member of the same congregation, challenged this notion that God could even be a "sadist." She exclaimed, "Whatever happens, God is not like us—and that should be enough!"

Frank, however, pressed on. "Well, we are supposed to be like God, and if we can see no good reason for wipeouts like this—none whatsoever—God must at least wonder about it, too. OK, maybe God is impotent or at least not an all-powerful Father."

Rabbi Harold Kushner said something similar in his famous book, *When Bad Things Happen to Good People*. He thought like this: maybe God could be infinitely good, but not infinitely powerful. God might not be able to stop much of the evil in the world because it happens outside the divine control. Yet we can believe that God is fully compassionate with those who suffer pain—from the slightest discomfort to the most excruciating agony. Those who sincerely call for help will be consoled.

Rabbi Kushner thinks God is all-good, but not all-powerful. Frank sometimes thinks God is all-powerful, but not all good. However, both men have to face big problems about whether "God is God." Neither of them seems to be able to keep together in his mind *both* the unlimited *power and* the unlimited *goodness* essential to the God of Jews, Christians, and Muslims.

All three theistic traditions regard divinity as *both unlimitedly* powerful *and unlimitedly* good. Frequently, their members speak about God being all-powerful and all-good. Yet *all*-good is not the same as *infinite*-good. *All* could mean something finite, referring to everything in the whole being, without meaning anything infinite.

Every good angel, for instance, is all-good. Being *all*-good is not really the same as being an actual *infinity of power and goodness*. Nonetheless, despite their troublesome wording sometimes, theists claim to believe in the absolute infinity or unlimitedness of God.

Some other religious traditions try to avoid the dilemma by going to the extent of denying that evil really exists. They seem to think, for instance, that a child who is crying from parental abuse is not really experiencing evil, but should grow in enlightenment about how the Absolute works its ways. This stoical perspective can be found in some form wherever the Absolute and its adversaries are regarded as impersonal forces.

For believers generally, evil can be regarded as whatever is wrong, bad, "inappropriate," or detracting from what is good. In any case, evil is quite real for people who are traditional Jews, Christians, and Muslims. These believers in a transcendent God are convinced that the responsibility for evil cannot be attributed reasonably or honestly to God.

At least, many do not hold God responsible for why the present world will eventually be destroyed. The evil prospects of the death of all living creatures and the total disintegration of the cosmos itself cannot be *specifically* caused by the divine. God will be ultimately responsible for a new heaven and for a new earth, but not for the ruination of the old and passing earth.

Traditional belief stands firmly against those who either deny the reality of evil or attribute even part of it to God. Theists believe in God as infinitely other than the world, but still somehow perfectly *within* it. God, they say, is both transcendent and immanent. They affirm the reality of evil, but assert that God did not create it as such.

God allows it. The *sole origin* of evil is believed to be within the free will of created persons.

The beginning of evil in the human world is thought to be the original disobedience and banishment of Adam and Eve. This first couple transmitted to every one of their descendants their own fallen condition. Whether it is taken literally or figuratively, the *Book of Genesis* reveals that we are all children of the same original parents who, by rebelling against God, spoiled the world into which we, their offspring, are conceived.

Adam and Eve were made in God's image and likeness, male and female (*Genesis* 1:27). But they really wanted to be more "like" God than they could possibly be. Eve told the serpent what God had commanded basically and yet she still chose to believe the lies of the tempter. She and Adam defied God by doing what was explicitly forbidden.

Many would say that this original disobedience was not an in-your-face opposition; it was rather disobedience of ignorance. After all, Adam and Eve did not blatantly hurl an epithet of hostility toward God as they bit into the forbidden fruit. Nevertheless, one has to admit that, by their deed and its rationalization, they were knowingly defying *God's* will.

Adam and Eve knew fully what they should never do, but they did it. Their ignorance was not about *how* to think and behave, but about *why*. Humility on their part could have led them eventually to come to know God's ways and reasons more fully, without resisting them.

Like many others, Rabbi Kushner lives in denial about the original disobedience. He has regarded this act as liberation from narrow adherence to "rules." He forgets that Adam and Eve disobeyed not only rules, but also the *person* of God. When a rule comes from a person who loves you and creates you "out of nothing" to be happy forever, your defiance constitutes a massive insult to the Giver and to yourself, the gift.

Others would like to think that the desire of Adam and Eve to be "more than human" could be an essential part of being human. That represents another ploy used to deflect our awareness away from God's knowledge, goodness, and power.

God knew what it is to be fully human, and thereby created Adam and Eve that way. God willed them to be human and only human, neither more nor less. However, they surely desired to be more than human. They did what God did not intend.

Adam and Eve did not simply choose to do their own thinking and behavior. They chose to become the *creators* of their values: to originate what their thinking and doing should ultimately *mean*. They chose to try to form their own morality, instead of choosing to let God determine *their* morality. We have obviously inherited the self-distorting results of their original choice.

The larger question, however, is rarely asked in polite company. *Why* did we inherit the sin of Adam and Eve—or, at least, why are we subject to its effects? Can the transmission of the transgression done by someone else account for why *we* live in this suffering and dying world?

Are we *really* innocent of our first parents' desire to be "more than human"? Or did we ourselves on our own—originally, fresh from the gift of being—take a like stance. If so, would we thereby *deserve* to receive the "eventual inheritance" of our prime offense and of its consequences by being generated within the cosmic prison?

Are we conceived in the space-time world such that we inherit not only the conditions and consequences of our first parents, but also something more? Perhaps we are also *self*-inheriting: inheriting the structure and the condition of being that comes directly from an *originative* offense of our own—a sin of self-deconstruction, and of damaging our whole being by abusing our own personal freedom at the moment of creation *out of nothing.*

How Could God Let Adam and Eve Do *This* to Us?

We can understand how Adam and Eve, by going against God, would bring suffering on themselves. Obviously, they were fully responsible for their own sin and its consequences for their lives. But how could an *unlimitedly* powerful and *unlimitedly* good God *allow* them to transmit the whole twisted condition to us?

Did God let us "get clunked" with the sin of someone else, without any freely determining act of participation on our own? An Islamic statement suggests that it could not be so. The *Quran* says that no one benefits except from his or her own works, and no one should bear the burden of another (6:164). Jews and Christians can read in *Ezekiel* 18:20-28 a similar intimation.

At least, if we think about it at all, we are likely to complain that, when we were conceived in this world, we did not get an "equal footing." Our original gifts from God appear to be arbitrary. None of the theistic traditions seems to explain this *initial disparity* in "gifts from God."

Original sin, for instance, is said to make *us necessarily* inclined to sin—to try to be more than human. However, if we were hit with this predisposition through no *personal* fault of our own, can that be divine justice? How much dignity and respect would God be giving each person, created in the likeness of God?

Besides, if God gives to some persons the kind of parents who are most diligent in teaching God's ways, while others are given parents who are dissolute or rebellious, is God being just or is God being arbitrary?

Since unlimited justice cannot be partial, the momentous question then surfaces. Are we *really innocent* victims of original sin—of an original radical tilt toward everlasting destruction?

The Blame Chain

According to the story in *Genesis*, God prohibited Adam and Eve from partaking of the tree of the knowledge of good and evil. For this "restriction" on individual choice, the serpent put the blame on God. With this premise of divine fault, the scheming tempter enticed our first parents. He urged them to throw off all limits and plunge into the unknown experience of *independence from* God.

They soon paid the price by being banished from closeness to God and from the perks of paradise. Before they begot us, they begot sin.

Does an inheritance of this sin—or, at least, of its consequences—adequately explain *why* we have to *enter this world*. Here we live a kind of existence that can torment us and will eventually put us to death.

If we *merely inherit* an original sin, then we are simply victims of our first parents. We can do nothing other than blame the *origin* of human evil on them directly. And we can indirectly—yet really and unconsciously—blame God for allowing this sin to be transmitted *unfreely* to us. In so doing, we are then no better than Adam who blamed Eve or Eve who blamed the serpent or the serpent who blamed God.

Adam almost seemed to be blaming God consciously by saying, "...The woman, whom thou gavest me to be my companion, gave me of the tree, and I did eat" (*Genesis* 3:12). He might have been blaming God for giving him *this* woman, and not a perfect one.

Should we really blame someone *else* for the *very beginning* of *our* plight? Granted, we are responsible for our own personal sins, committed once we have participated in this world. Nevertheless, have we no responsibility for coming to *exist* in this *suffering kind* of world? Does not Eve need to take responsibility for her choice? Adam, for his choice? And what about us, were we without any *original*, *personal* choice or *freedom* of will?

Consider Alan and Stephanie, the highly distraught parents whose noticeable negligence crushed their son to death. Was not each of them responsible in his or her own way for what happened to the child?

What can be said about Johnny himself? He did not seem to have any choice at all. His own father killed him before he could do much. Did God allow this to happen to him unjustly or was Johnny also *somehow* responsible for what happened—for existing in that condition of high vulnerability? Did Alan and Stephanie "kill" their offspring in likeness to Adam and Eve "killing" us?

We ought to examine ourselves carefully. Before our entry into this world, did we somehow have a primal choice of our own? Did we engage in an original act of self-determination that we are now concealing from ourselves? Is there at least some sense to thinking that we have deserved what we inherited? Should we, too, take responsibility, and let ourselves be truly liberated from this chain of blame?

Perhaps one of the main reasons for even being in this kind of world is the opportunity to become aware, and to repent, of an as-yet-repressed sin. This act of sin would have been committed at the moment we were created "out of nothing." And that moment was *not* at conception, where we were created by means of a sperm and ovum of our father and mother.

All repression involves unconscious denial. Are we, perhaps, even now unconsciously denying that anything like this *could* be real?

Is the Blame Chain Breakable?

Our contemporary psychoanalytic culture has immersed us in the blame chain. Psychologists and psychiatrists like to trace emotional problems to defects in our parents. Then, of course, our parents' problems can be traced further back to defects in their parents and grandparents. Knowing where problems of abuse originated in the family can help with healing. Yet this psychosocial chain leads all the way back to Adam and Eve.

Perhaps we ought to start asking *why* we became children of Adam and Eve in the first place. Why did we not perhaps become children of some other "first parents," who did not sin? Is God restricted to creating only the world that is now most immediately evident to us—the one marked by space and time in which we find ourselves? Is the human community—as we have come to know it—the only "community" of humans?

Maybe there are other humans who do not have a background of disobedience to God. In such a case, there would be no reason for them to be in our kind of world—a world requiring redemption from sin by the means of parenthood and so much more.

Multitudes of Christians believe that we who are inhabiting the earth were conceived in original sin. As a result, we were destined for everlasting alienation from heaven unless God were to send us a Savior, who is Jesus Christ. Jews and Muslims also believe that only God can rescue us, even though they do not claim that we were "conceived in sin" or that Jesus has the decisive role as Savior.

Whatever we believe about salvation, we still might wonder. Were there other *human* persons, created with us "out of nothing," who remained sinless. Such humans would not become descendants of Adam and Eve, nor would they inherit original sin. These human persons would have said fully *yes* to God and thereby never have become *fallen* persons like *us*.

The Bible, for instance, refers to good and bad angels. According to the common interpretation of the Christian Testament, Lucifer rebelled against God, and so did a third of the angelic hosts with him (*Revelation* 12:4,9). Yet two thirds apparently said fully *yes* to God.

Why the Bible does not mention even the possibility of a similar, original division of will among humans is not the real question. The Bible affords us knowledge for salvation, but there are many things about God and creation that it does not reveal—at least not overtly.

The main issue, at this point, is simple. Is it *possible* that we are personally responsible for the consequences of original sin—along with Adam and Eve—even though we are not responsible for the "Garden Sin" itself? Did God simply impose original sin—or at least its massive consequences—on free, individual persons like us, without our having personal responsibility in any way?

Or was the *original* sin of Adam and Eve the *prime symptom* of an *originative* sin, committed by them *and by us* in the non-temporal moment of universal creation "out of nothing"? We know God is *infinitely* powerful and also *infinitely* good. God is infinitely loving, just, compassionate, and merciful. So, could God have "stood by" while we were smitten with the consequences of someone else's sin *that we did not deserve*?

When we really think we are innocent victims of original sin, then we seem to be deeply involved in blaming God for subjecting us to undeserved torments. People today, for instance, contemplating the Holocaust, are tempted either to blame God or to disbelieve in God entirely.

If we blame God, however, we are going back to the traditionally unacceptable interpretations of divinity. These elucidations say that there are limits to either divine power or divine goodness. The only alternative to this kind of blaming, then, would be to say that God is not at fault because God can do or be whatever God *wants*. But that supposition necessarily makes of God a (potential) tyrant or a bully. Besides, with God, there are no *wants*. God does not want (lack) anything. With God, everything is *will*: *infinitely free goodness* of will.

The God believed by theists—Jews, Christians, and Muslims—is not an arbitrary Will. God's will is infinitely true, wise, and good. Truth, wisdom, and goodness are not really arbitrary properties of an irrational Will. They are the eternal character traits of an infinitely *perfect*, superabundantly loving, personal Being. (Strictly speaking, the word "perfect" would apply literally to the fullness of a positive process—"*per-facere*," to make thoroughly—and not to God whose being is without process. However, the perennial usage of the word *perfect* has overridden this implication. Therefore, we will use the word as meaning *flawless*, with no process implied, whether the perfect one at issue is finite or infinite.)

God can also be said to be infinite "integrity"—*unlimited harmony* of truth, goodness, beauty, wisdom, freedom, and the rest. God's infinite power and goodness are infinitely confluent.

We must face squarely the classic dilemma that comes from minds fixated on *either-or*. In view of evil being done to innocent children and others, God is often thought to be *either* infinitely powerful and somewhat cruel *or* infinitely good and somewhat weak.

We might think like Frank, the disillusioned Christian. Then we would have to agree that God would allow *innocent* persons to be tortured by the sin of their first parents. We are then regarding God as, at least partly, sadistic.

Or else, trying to be on God's side, so to speak, we might prefer to think, as many do, that God is weak, rather than cruel. Then we would be making God out to be a Supreme Big Daddy, who thinks "his kids" are originally blameless and wants to give them all the best, but is not "the most powerful daddy on the block." Such a God is unable to prevent either evil forces or mere chance from ravaging his family. Evil is then more powerful than God.

These opposing interpretations of God—as sadist or big daddy—are two extreme ways to deny *our* originative sin. They amount to avenues by which we attempt to deny *our own responsibility for being in this kind of world*. Nonetheless, traditional theists, have always believed that God is *both* infinitely powerful *and* infinitely good. They do not abandon their *both-and* mentality.

Suppose then that we really believe in the absolutely unlimited power, unlimited goodness, and unconditional divine love. We have only one way to go in order to discover the source of our slavery to sin and its effects—all of them. We have to turn to *ourselves*, and not simply to Adam and Eve. We have to get real.

Our every pain in this world could be then understood as a mild shock wave coming out from under a Great Repression. We could be repressing our personal share of involvement in the very *origin* of evil—at the creation of being *out of nothing*.

From childhood into adulthood, we might have been conditioned by this world's dullness to deny unconsciously that we have "run over" our innermost Child. Perhaps, through cultural conditioning, we are holding ourselves back from acknowledging the shock that *caused* a lifetime—our present lifetime. In this life, we are hoping for relief from our pain, doubt, fear, and eventual death that might ultimately have been caused by *our very first response* to God—now buried in our spiritual unconsciousness.

Entering into our own being, then, might be the only way to break the chain of blame. We could be called to uncover an original, now-unconscious denial on *our* part. Yet we are quite unaware of being present when evil got started. How then could we be even partly responsible for its *origin*?

Perhaps it might be rewarding to make some extra effort to see ourselves and divine Revelation further from within. What might be "the inside story"?

Chapter 2

How in the World Did We Get *Here*?

"I've got enough guilt as it is; don't suggest any more!" That is the way Helen, a divorced mother of several children, reacted when she was first confronted with the prospect of our having committed an *originative* sin. She shrunk from the possibility that we might be responsible even for the bad things that *happen to* us, and that we do not know it consciously. Immediately repelled and threatened, she did not even want to know whether it was true or false.

We can sympathize with Helen. Guilt *feelings* can overwhelm our capacity for guilt *meanings*. Our search, however, is not for guilt feelings, but for any possible guilt *meanings*. And in order to attain perspective, we only need to look carefully into our own past record of denying choices that we have made.

Repression occurs when we fail to acknowledge something and do not *allow* ourselves to be conscious that we know it. We do not *let* ourselves know that we know it.

Some of our decisions are too painful to remember. Therefore, we protect ourselves from the pain by blanking them out. In addition, we shy away from recalling embarrassing experiences, even in the little things of ordinary life.

So it is not surprising that we fail to wonder about how we got into this world—a world of trivia and terror, of boredom and brilliance. We *assume* that we have no *personal* responsibility for being here.

We experience the inherent confinement of space and time. But we do not question the accompanying result: our massively enfeebled freedom. We do not realize that even the freest persons in our world are operating at a modest level of self-determination and potential.

Every day we are dealing with *conscious* decisions. So, we find it difficult to discern some of our most unconscious commitments.

And we can even think that repression has been minimal so far in our lives. We can repress our repressions.

We might not be able to recall actual instances when we have repressed some feeling, meaning, or fact of this world. Nevertheless, we only have to realize how readily we *are capable* of doing so. We can repress the truth about ourselves in actions of widely varying magnitude. We are can bury alive ideas and experiences without any conscious attention. A heartrending happening might occasion deep repression and forgetfulness. An example might serve to dramatize and symbolize this possibility.

A Wake-Up Call

Steven was an intelligent, sociable college student, likeable and generous with his family and friends. A bright career was looming because of his attractive personality and success in his studies.

Then one night he went to a party. It was his 21st birthday. Hosted by friends, the festive mood started rather early in the evening. His companions began encouraging him to indulge in the "spirits." After all, they said, he was, at last, fully an adult.

As each new friend or group stopped in and a round of drinks was served, Steven participated. When he finally began to hesitate, his companions assured him good-naturedly by saying that he was now a "man" and could hold his own on this special occasion, his first day as an "adult."

The morning after the party, however, Steven awoke with a severe headache. As he gradually gained consciousness, he became aware of the different pattern of light at the window. Instead of seeing horizontal lines of light and shadow like the venetian blinds in his bedroom, he saw vertical lines.

Then it dawned on him. He was not at home. Those were bars on the window. And the door side of the room was barred as well. He was in jail.

As he wondered where he was and why he was there, someone came to the door of the cell. Steven had a vague notion he knew the person, but he could not be sure. The visitor assured him, however, that she was his friend, Maria.

Steven asked, "Why am I here in jail, and how did I get here?"

Maria replied, "Steve, don't you remember? Last night at your birthday party you had a lot to drink. When you drove home, you struck three people walking along the side of the road. Two are dead, and one is in the hospital seriously injured."

At that point, Steven did not remember, and he was challenged to accept on faith that he was justly confined in jail.

The morning after the birthday, there he was...unaware of his original self-negation in taking too many of the drinks offered the night before. By his own personal freedom, he had put himself into a condition of enslavement to himself and to society. It was not a good way to begin his "adult life."

Over several months, with the assistance of friends and a special counselor, he came to realize what he had done, and he accepted its consequences. He gradually developed at least some recognition of the enormity of his actions, done while he was celebrating entry into the world of adult responsibilities.

Moreover, Steven *repented*. He did not continue his repression. He acknowledged his personal responsibility for an overindulgence in himself by succumbing to the pressures of human respect and the momentary pleasures of excessive drinking.

Steven was bitterly aware of his own impotence to compensate adequately the afflicted families of the injured and deceased. He nevertheless began paying for some of the damages. He made a commitment to offer long-term compensation once he attained an ongoing income. He also desired personally to console the family members, as best he could.

But suppose that Steven had refused to repent and to make some kind of restitution. Assume that he declined to forgive both himself and the friends who had goaded him on. Then his tragedy would have been compounded for the rest of his life. If he were *unwilling* to accept personal responsibility for the event that had incarcerated him, he would thereby have further alienated himself—from himself and from the human community.

Suppose We Messed Up and Blanked Out

Through this painful incident from ordinary life, Steven can speak to us. We are now confined within the cosmic world of heartache, sickness, and death. We might have to acknowledge our personal responsibility for having come to be here. Can we continue to go along in this world of fortune and misfortune, while assuming that we and our fellow travelers, are *originally* innocent of it all? Perhaps we ought to wonder seriously whether we are responsible for some kind of wrong turn at the *origin* of our personal *being*.

At least, in humility like Steven, we might begin to consider this serious possibility of faith: are we somehow *personally* responsible for having inherited original sin and its imprisoning effects? Is our "lockup" in cosmic confinement somehow a matter of justice?

We might simply ask "What if?" What if we deserve to be in this world where, inevitably, bad things happen as well as good things? Some might wonder how they ever "deserved" to be in a world as *good* as this one. Even so, they might be sensing a deep sinfulness in themselves: their own personal fault for being in a world that seems too good for them. Most folks, however, do not recognize much sin and are simply perplexed about all the suffering we must do.

Like a scientific hypothesis, this faith-proposal about our personal responsibility might not be held to be certainly true, but it could be a meaningful consideration. Such a perspective might lead us into new and deeper meaning for life. We might ask, simply and seriously, "What if it is true that you and I were freely involved in a primordial catastrophe that we have totally buried alive as if it did not happen?"

The question itself could help us to see this world within a more revealing light. We could discover something new about our radical need for healing from God.

Looking for Clues

Suppose we were detectives trying to solve a murder case with a few possible suspects. We would be seriously challenged to find the *real* culprit. Even though, from the present evidence, one of them seems least likely to be the killer, that particular suspect still must be checked out. We might have to surmise how he or she could have done it—even though it seems like an outlandish construction. Then we would have to look for clues and test this projected possibility by the most forceful analysis of the facts in the case.

Similarly, we could try to determine who is chiefly responsible for the *origin* of evil within our lives. Could it be God, Adam and Eve, Satan, cosmic matter, or each one of us free creatures? We would even have to entertain seriously the possibility that each one of us children of Adam and Eve is somehow responsible.

We cannot always, of course, discern which person causes any specific evil in *this* world. But we could consider the moment of our being created, whole and perfect "out of nothing." In *responding immediately* to God, each person could have freely caused some pristine good, but also some original evil. Consequently, he or she *necessarily* would have become subject to the present world with its alternating good and bad, beauty and ugliness.

How, then, can we say that we got here in this world? We *caused ourselves* to *be* here; but we also must have caused the *here* to *be*. With multitudes of other "hesitators in being," we contributed to the coming to be of a polluted existence—part of which is known as the *cosmos*.

A painful, self-inflicted wound, one that is as deep as the roots of our *existence* in this universe, could be buried deep within us. We ourselves might have done something wrong that might be even deeper and darker than the sin of Adam and Eve in Eden.

The latter sin started the succession of human lives in space and time. An *originative* sin, however, on the part of each of us, along with Adam and Eve, made this kind of life in the spatiotemporal world *necessary*.

Tragedies like that of Alan running over and killing his own child while blaming "the kids" might reveal something. We might be reminded, ever so slightly, how we hide from ourselves our original act of *being* ourselves—how we "run over" it.

Our First Response to God's Gift

We could call our pristine personal act of freedom our "primal choice" or our "original will." This act of will would have been a frontal, immediate response to God's act of creating us. Moreover, the act of God, to which we would have been responding, would have to have been a *perfect* act.

All of God's acts are *infinitely* perfect. The act of *creation* brought persons into being. These created persons were finitely *perfect*—the only kind of creatures God *could* create *out of nothing*. A less-than-perfect condition would not be the result of *God's* power and intent.

At first, we might have trouble with the idea. But we might be overlooking the obvious: *God* could not create *directly* an imperfect creature or an imperfect freedom any more than a square circle, a male mother, or a puppet saint. God *could only* create directly *perfect finite* beings. Anyone who might think that God could create *immediately out of nothing* any being that is simply good, but not perfect, is demeaning the *infinity* of God's power and goodness. Subtly perhaps, such a person would be regarding God as a mega-creature—a Mega-Maker, not an infinite Creator.

Most people think God can *directly* create *imperfect* beings, such as elephants or drops of water. They are confusing limited being with imperfect being. Being limited or finite is not the same as being imperfect, even though every imperfect being, such as everything that is in the physical world, is a finite being.

The first creatures of *God* would have to be persons with *perfect freedom*. And the first exercise of their freedom would be their *immediate* response to the gift of their own being and to God, the Giver of that being. This response would be one that is perfectly free and not constricted by circumstances that might inhibit this freedom. Such freedom would not be subject to any qualification, such as a temptation. It would be the exercise of pure, *untemptable* freedom.

This first free response to *being* would be made by limited beings with perfect finite freedom. It would be quite different from what has been called the original choice of our first parents. By *their* choice, we eventually entered the functionally defective world of space and time. Theirs was a tempted choice: temptation-*full*. Their originative act of will, of hesitation to *be*, had made them temptable.

The first act of our *being*—and of the *being* of Adam and Eve—would have to be done free of the confines of a "Garden" or of any space and time. It would be the perfectly free personal response to

God's Person-to-person act of creating us "out of nothing." Not out of dust or a rib, or out of the gametic cells of a mother and father. Pristine creation would not be conditioned by passive matter or a subject of any kind. It would be strictly *ex nihilo*—out of nothing, conditioned by nothing. Fully interpersonal.

The *power* to exercise our originative response to being-at-all was the absolute *gift* of God to us. But this gift of perfect *power*—perfect freedom to respond fully—is not at all the same as the first *act* of that power. The *act* of immediately responding, on our part, would be *our* inherently free response to the gift of our own being. Granted what we know of ourselves now, that *act* must have been less than perfect—something that we are spiritually repressing.

This prime *act* of self-determination was "fresh out of nothing," independent of time, space, and other conditioning. As a hesitation to *be*, it would have been a free act of violating our own freedom as we were brought to *be*. We did this original violation of our freedom apparently along with the freedom failures of multitudes of other perfect persons, angelic and human.

At the interpersonal moment that God said, "Be," we would have failed to receive well the limited, yet *perfect*, being with which we were being gifted. Our defective response would have *caused*, within us, a personal and communal implosion. Our being would have become flat, fractured, and fragmented—becoming limp and seeming more like the nothingness "from which we came" than like God.

Even the *slightest* hesitation to affirm *fully* the gift of our perfect being and to praise the infinite goodness of the Giver would have to yield devastating consequences. After all, the perfect gift of *being*—of creation—comes by the activity of the *infinitely* loving heart of God. The crash of our being would have been entirely *self*-caused.

Nevertheless, God is now acting to restore us. After the crash, our eventual conception and growth within the passively material world already marks a significant measure of partial recovery from our self-inflicted emptiness. We are well on the way, but with a long row to hoe.

Like Alan, contemplating his son's crushed body, we might now be experiencing a world that has resulted from our own and others' original carelessness. In doing our *act* of *be*-ing—in *exercising* our perfect *power* of freedom, we—not our power—said less than fully *yes*. Part of the compensating result is the wake-up world of matter, motion, space, and time. Yet we still cannot admit that this world is the broken child of our being's first act of freedom.

We have been taught that the origin of sin is in us because we are in the community of Adam and Eve. This is quite true. Eventually, however, we might have to acknowledge that it is *much truer to say* that we are in the community of Adam and Eve *because of* how our sinfulness absolutely *originated in us*. We are not sinners so much because we are in the community of Adam and Eve, but we are in their community because we are sinners.

Besides, if we are to recover from our own being's semi-collapse of freedom, only God's infinitely merciful love can save us. We can be full of hope for God's restoration. Our redemption has already been attained. Now we look to salvation, to our *receiving genuinely* this redemptive love.

In our anxiety, even a sincere *nod* to God would be enough to start the process of personal salvation. God might be our *personal* Savior in a depth we have hardly suspected.

Chapter 3

Freedom's Wider World

Our present conditions of existence blare the "news" that we are all recovering from a fall. Through growth and development, trial and error, and hopeful successes we are making an attempt to recover.

Yet how was this fall *ours* at all? Were we somehow dropped? Or pushed? Did the devil do it to us? If so, God is not God: infinitely good, infinitely powerful, infinitely protective of what is true, good, and beautiful.

Are we perhaps personally responsible for a wrong "choice" at the beginning of our *being*? Did we somehow *will* ourselves into this condition? Are we here because we abused the gift of our freedom?

If so, such a partial failure in first exercising our perfect freedom would have to have occurred at the beginning of our *being*—not at the beginning of our *becoming.* This act could not have been done in space and time, nor with Adam and Eve in Eden.

No, this absolutely first act of self-direction could have been done only *at the supreme moment of being-at-all—at our creation out of nothing.* By an act of receiving *less than perfectly* the gift of who we are, we fell. *We* caused the crash and the need for our recovery. In order to realize what happened to our *being*, we would have to begin our *becoming*, our *coming* alive, through natural and supernatural means.

The Light of Primary Truths

As we test this new perspective, we can begin to base the case on some critically important truths that have been cherished by Jews, Christians, and Muslims. The most important truths are, on the one hand, the infinite goodness and infinite power of God; and, on the other hand, the pure freedom of self-determination of the individual human person. God can save us. But only if we freely cooperate.

If we actually did mess up our act of first freedom and blanked out, we would now be profoundly numb to primal truths. We would be barely able to appreciate God's *infinite* love and power, as well as the presumed gift of our *perfect* freedom. Our recognition would be only vague, like that of drunks recovering from a hangover.

We might *assert* that we believe God's goodness and power are infinite and that, in being gifts of God, we are free. Nevertheless, we might not really understand the words we are using. We might be thinking of infinite reality rather as grand indefiniteness—not really *unlimited* at all. In addition, our freedom might be considered to be merely a freedom of choice among set alternatives rather than a pure act of self-determination.

We need to think soberly and carefully. The Scriptural revelation concerning Adam and Eve might be more than the story of a first ill-choosing couple. This revelation might imply something concerning our primary, immediate, and supremely free response to the gift of *being*—and to God, the Gifter.

Traditionally, theists believe in God as wholly *other than* creation. They know God as one who *gifts* someone to be "out of nothing." There is no pre-existing stuff. God is not like created creators who must have something with which to work. God brings each being to *be out of nothing*, gifted with an uniquely perfect personal freedom. Moreover, God *freely* creates. Creation is not a "necessity."

Original Freedom

So, the new point of view takes seriously this creation "out of nothing." Its supposition would be that God, an infinitely perfect Creator, created whole, perfect creatures. God's act of creation was *inter*personal. The creatures had to be persons; they were gifted with their own perfect, finite freedom in order to respond immediately. How could *God* gift them with *anything* imperfect?

As *persons*, these created ones were complete in their natures and powers. Their *being-created* was not at all a conception or birth in this space-time world of *inherent* imperfection. And in the very act of *being-created*, each one, necessarily and freely, gave a reception to the gift of their *being*—and to their essence as being *this* or *that* unique person.

At the moment of the creation, God said, "Be." And each one of these free human persons responded immediately to the gift of being in one of three ways: positively with gratefulness, negatively with rebellion, or "hesitantly" with reservations. Each might have said, person-to-Person, to their person-all Creator—immediately and with perfect freedom—*yes*, *no*, or *maybe*.

Those who responded with an unreserved *yes* must have entered heaven immediately. They fulfilled perfectly their perfect freedom. Multitudes of angels apparently said *yes*. Perhaps countless human persons—persons of purely active matter and spirit—also said fully *yes* and never had to become members of Adam's "fallen human race." Such persons were not thereby subjected to the *redemptive condition* of *passive* matter and *passive* spirit that *we* have to endure.

Those who said an outright *no* thereby plunged themselves into an absolute failure forever—known as hell. They entirely frustrated their own perfect freedom. Lucifer and multitudes of angelic beings apparently made this primal act of self-determination. It is likely that there were humans who did so, too.

Those who freely "hesitated"—those saying *yes-and-no* (in effect, *maybe*)—must have caused themselves to enter into some kind of structural shock: the trauma of a failure adequately to be, to *do* their being. Their *maybe*, while it said a partial *yes*, also said a partial *no* to the *gift* of being and to their Creator.

By their initial reservation about being-at-all, these *maybe*-sayers deformed their own being. But they did not destroy themselves.

By freely acting with the very being itself that they were given, these *semi-yes*-sayers chose somewhat weakly to affirm who and what they are. In perfect freedom, they caused themselves to be imperfect beings. They violated—but did not destroy—their God-gifted freedom to be. As *gifted* by God, they remained perfect. As *received* immediately and freely by themselves, they were imperfect.

As *maybe*-sayers, they partly disowned the incomparable gift of being-at-all. *They freely failed to affirm fully that they were perfect creatures of God.* Their very denial *caused* them to *be imperfect*.

Their faltering might also explain some other key realities: why they had to have parents and eventually to be conceived within this world of good and evil (of *yes* and *no*), why they had to inherit the sin of their first parents, and why they could not possibly be free of unhappiness.

They are we. When God said *be*, we said *maybe*. This "maybe" was not a mere external word such as we experience in the present world. This "saying" was a doing, a meaning, and even a *be*-ing: a stance of our whole selves by which we freely responded with a somewhat indifferent attitude to God and to the gift of be-ing.

Because of a partial *yes* in our *maybe*—*maybe* we will fully affirm the goodness of being—we remained beautiful creatures of God. Yet there was a partial *no* in our *maybe*—*maybe* we will deny entirely the goodness of being. We thereby required the ministry of a space-time (gradual) form of being (an *exist*-ence) in order to move toward repentance and into a complete *yes*, through the saving power of God.

Our denial is so massive that even now we commonly think of existence (*ex-sistere*, to stand outside) as equivalent to *being*. We even say that God *exists*, rather than simply, "God *is*." But God *is*, without any "standing outside self" manner of being—without any *existence*.

Strictly speaking, then, God does not *exist*. God *is*. We have projected onto God *our* kind of being—a self-defective manner of being, an *existing*.

In other words, by the first and most free kind of act that we could ever do, we freely failed to receive fully the gift of *who* we are. Consequently, the *no*-power in this first act of our free will must have deformed the structure and paralyzed the function of our very *being* itself. God certainly did not do it; nor could God *let* any other created person do it *to* us. By freely, yet defectively, doing our *be*-ing, we entered upon *existence*—a manner of being "out of it."

We have blinded ourselves against realizing our *self-inflicted* punishment. We are inclined to think that if we had a perfectly free, unclouded choice, we would be present directly to the infinite glory of God. We assume then that we would be unable to refuse God when faced with the divine glory. We think we would not be able to say *no*. We imagine that the infinite power and goodness of God would overwhelm us.

But this is to misunderstand. God's power is infinite. Hence, it is *infinitely receptive* of *our* freedom and could interfere *in no way* with its fullest exercise. Once a creature in perfect finite freedom said *fully yes*, that affirmation itself would be what *let in*—let into the creature—the infinite glory of God forever.

God *forces* no one in any way—neither in creation nor in heaven. Even in heaven, God's glory does not *force* persons. Rather they come completely free into the divine presence, having confirmed themselves within the gift of being by saying fully *yes*. In heaven, persons *could* not say *no* because they *would* not say *no*. By God's *grace* of *creation,* the power of self-determination gifts them. Once they exercise their *be*-ing *perfectly*, they do so perfectly forever. For Christians, at least, heaven is a fully free union of infinitely free Persons with finite and fully free persons.

We imperfect lovers are beset by a fixation on the spatial and the temporal—conditions that we helped to cause. We constantly think and talk as though eternity itself was some kind of a *very* long time. We do not recognize that temporal life is a real, but distorted, *way of relating* to eternity.

Eternity is the way of *infinite* being *only*. There is no beginning and no end. Eternity is *non*-durational. Time, however, is a real, experiential, defective condition *within* eternity—without being any "part" of it. *Forever* is real, and not a "very long time," but the perfectly natural way for a finite *person* to be—with an absolute beginning and definitely no end.

Infinite freedom and goodness *could not* overwhelm free creatures who are exercising personal freedom perfectly. Only created persons who say less than fully *yes* would render themselves subject to being "overwhelmed" by infinitely intimate Love.

At the non-durational moment of being created we were fully in the presence of divine Being, fully and immediately free, to say yes; but not yet bathed in the Glory.

In those who say *fully yes*, their receptively good will makes it possible to receive the infinite *glory* of God. They actually receive consummate joy, without being overpowered at all.

God is not *blinding* light, but *infinitely-enabling* light. God is the benign radiance of infinite love—unimaginable to us *self-darkened* creatures. God never incapacitates. Only we, within our own present blindness, project onto God the attribute of a radiating glory that overpowers.

Indecisive Freedom

Our *originative* act of freedom must have been fresh and perfectly free—either decisive or decisively indecisive. In no way could it have been the result of a halting, mistake-prone *deliberation*, such as we undergo in *this* world. The empirical world is the *consequence* of our original degree of *willingness to be less* than who and what we were gifted to be.

The indecisive kind of freedom that we experience here in this life begins to reflect an originally decisive *indecisiveness*. We must have engaged in the decisive, though partial, rejection of the infinitely intimate act of *creation*—infinitely giftive *and infinitely receptive*—by which we were gifted to *be*.

The slightest free "indecision" in responding instantly to God and to the gift of being would *necessarily create* a gap. Our relationship with God would incur a necessary rupture that we ourselves could never heal. Only the infinitely merciful love of God could make it *possible* for us to be restored. There would have to be both a kind of "re-creativity" on God's part and an eventual change of heart on our part.

By our participation in the world of space and time, as well as in the world of spirit, God would gradually enable us to remove the *no* from our first act of freedom, our *maybe*. We would be required somehow to submit: to repent and to give our permission for the removal of our *no* and its effects.

By our partly-*no*, first *act* of *be*-ing, we would have rendered our freedom quite imperfect. We would no longer have the power of perfect functional freedom. Consequently, we would not be able to "save ourselves" from being *forever* alienated from God and from our true selves.

Our *power* of freedom in the originative creation "out of nothing" had to be perfect and full. The *power* was perfect and a sheer gift of God. But the *act* of that power of *freedom* was our gift and not God's. In our *first act*, the slightest failure of our will to love God perfectly therein would be a mortal miscarriage of justice and love. Such an act would leave us dangling between heaven and hell. Even as it is now, in this space-time world of Adam and Eve, our freest acts are burdened with our self-centered desires and our relative blindness to truth in action.

In our present world of "hang-ups," the slight failures of will, such as neglecting to check out thoroughly all alternatives for an action, might seem to be only small transgressions. They stem, however, from our common *capacity* to engage in more serious matters of choosing poorly: such as murder, extortion, adultery. Petty theft is far from grand larceny; but it is a beginning. All of our failures of will flow from the originative theft of praise for God.

Suppose that *not a single one* of God's lovingly created persons had violated the perfect gift of freedom. Suppose that every created person—angelic and human—had said *freely* and *fully yes.*

If the initial, self-inflicted bad *will* had not occurred in anyone, then one thing can be said definitely and surely. There would be *no suffering at all in any being anywhere*. Only heaven. No space and time. No becoming and healing. Pure bliss everlasting in perfect freedom and love.

All finite persons, by their free and full *yes* to being, would have freely entered forever into ecstatic communion with God. Each one would have given a full-hearted response to the gift of being-at-all. Thereby they would have received fully the infinitely perfect act of God bringing each being to be. Together all persons would have co-created a perfect union of joy and communion forever.

Such is not the case. Our free *un*willingness to give a full response to our Creator must have originated the partial disposition toward evil that we find within our being. We caused or "created" our need for the present kind of world—a profound *mix* of good and evil.

Here we encounter the effects of our own unwillingness, endure them, and hope for a Savior.

If we *maybe*-sayers are somewhat open-minded and openhearted, we can be brought to admit something awesome. Despite a lack of being clearly conscious of *what* we did to ourselves, we must say that we are freely and decisively at fault for being in this world. We deserve to be subject to the consequences of our own incipient act of will. We were immediately, freely, and decisively willing to be less than full-hearted lovers of God. This partial kind of willingness has resulted, as a whole, in our existing as less than perfect persons.

Consequently, we can be known to be, even now, *both* perfect *and* imperfect. Perfect as gifted by God, and imperfect as received by ourselves. By our own imperfection, however, we do not destroy the perfection of originative being with which God has gifted us. Our imperfection is an "add on" to our perfection, not a destruction or a removal of it. We are really not simplistically imperfect as opposed to perfect. We are paradoxically imperfect by being *both* perfect *and* imperfect. We are not *simply* perfect. Nor simply imperfect.

Our fixation on ourselves and our space-time, empirical concerns binds us to thinking that all beings—including spiritual ones—are *either* perfect *or* imperfect and cannot be both. But beings that are strictly and solely imperfect—molecules, plants, animals, *et al.*—are found only in the cosmos and its environs of inherently passive and intrinsically imperfect reality.

Our Freedom Here and Now

Even in everyday life, we recognize that we are individually free to some extent. In spite of physical and emotional constraints, we are still free to decide what *attitude* we will take toward anything and everything.

Suppose two thugs are beating you to death. As long as you are conscious, you are free to bless or curse your persecutors.

You might adopt an attitude that says, "If I somehow get out of this situation I will go after you and even your children." You might have a vengeful attitude, a malicious personal determination.

Or you might adopt an attitude that says, "I am sorry you are doing this, both for what it is doing to me and for what it is doing to *you*. You really do not know what you are doing. It is terribly wrong, but I am surely willing to forgive you." Your attitude would be one of love and forgiveness. It might even be heroic or saintly.

Your attitude, of course, could be somewhere between these two "extremes." But it would be *your* attitude and would show right here and now—at least to you and to God—what kind of *human* person you *intend* to be. There might be many restrictions on your freedom of movement and feeling—you could not help feeling pain and anger. But your freedom to determine your attitude would remain.

This kind of freedom means something paradoxical. Fallen human persons are limited in what they can *do or accomplish*. But they are not practically limited in how good or bad as persons they can *be*. By the pivotal *attitude* willed at any given moment, each person is somewhat freely determining his or her quality of being a human person.

Even as we are now, the very root of human freedom constitutes a natural capacity. We are able freely to accept or reject—in attitude and action—the unlimited power and goodness of God.

This radical capacity is likewise the ability freely to accept or to reject our physical, emotional, and spiritual abilities, disabilities, and liabilities. Even the sincere, if only slight, *intent* to receive God's unconditional love can be a decisive beginning for recovery. God's infinitely healing love can "do the rest." There is no simplistic, one-to-one correlation between the meaning of our acts as performed in space and time and the meaning of our acts relative to eternity.

Every day we have many conditions of limitation and constriction on freedom. But these are opportunities to say, spiritually, *yes* or *no*. Much of the time we are, at best, willing to say *maybe*. Our attitudes of impatience amply demonstrate this weakness.

Human freedom is the power of self-determination. We can be a *yes*, *no*, or *maybe* kind of person. But sin has already damaged our freedom. This critical self-impairment might even be called the *sin of maybe*.

Whose sin did the *decisive* damaging? Who is responsible for the functional maiming, such that each one has been conceived and born alienated from God? Is Adam responsible? Eve? The serpent? God? They all *seem* responsible *if* we were *forced* either to inherit what someone else did wrong or to suffer its consequences.

Most people never entertain the possibility that *they and the rest of us* are the principal causes of the *origin* of sin in our lives. They *repress* it. Moreover, if it would cross their minds as even remotely plausible, they are willing to *suppress* it for the sake of blaming Adam and Eve. They are willing to take for granted the origin of the process of redemption. They are willing to let Adam and Eve be the prime lawbreakers. Such a primal position of being (or attitude) is convenient and outwardly comfortable.

The wiles of Lucifer also bear in upon us as we live in this world. His twisted thrusts of "light bearing" darkness are a grave danger to our everlasting destiny. Therefore, we are quite ready to blame the evil one. We think Lucifer is far more responsible than we are for our basic predicament and for how we came to be within this world. Perhaps our complacency is quite compatible with his present intent for us.

God Respects Our Freedom

In creation, we could not fundamentally determine who or what we are—whether angelic or human. Only the Creator determines that. Yet in giving us a free, self-determining kind of (human) being, the Creator would have to respect freedom—ours and that of the divine Wisdom as well.

Suppose that, *at the time of conception within our mothers*, we had *no* responsibility for the conflict and offensiveness into which we were entering. Still, would not an infinitely just and merciful God then ask our permission before allowing us to be afflicted? Could God allow us—from this "absolute" beginning—to be clobbered by grave imperfection of structure and deformation of function? Does not God respect the created person's integrity of freedom?

Many theologians today, however, conclude that God deliberately created us imperfect. They like to surmise that we must have been given a flawed freedom. Within this condition, we would have to struggle in order to become virtuous. Some would assert that this is why we are the subject of evolution.

But such is clearly a projection of what *we* might do if *we* were the Creator.

We think of finite persons as having to "earn" whatever is good for them. We think that it is "the way of God." While such servile kind of thinking might apply, in some ways, to *redemptive creation*, it is absurd when applied to our *originative relationship* with God.

Everything God gives is done unconditionally and perfectly. God says, "Be free," and means it. God's gift-giving is not something petty; it is unlimitedly generous. No strings are attached. Only our miserly ways as fallen creatures would prompt us to think of such a "divine arrangement": work first, reward later.

So, if the free creature were to be subject to injustice from the start, only two possibilities could really account for it. Either such a creature did not cause the injustice, but agrees freely to suffer for others, or else the creature caused the injustice itself, along with others, and deserves to suffer the consequences.

God might have asked one of those created human persons who said fully *yes* to help in the redemption of the *maybe*-sayers. This chosen one (or more) could be asked to suffer with us who deserve the experiences of pain and anguish in a life of cosmic confinement. Such a sinless creature, living among us sinners, would be an unique light shining in the darkness.

This chosen redemption-helper would have already said, at the moment of creation, fully and unconditionally, *yes* to God. So, to the divine offer to be such a helper, a cooperative *yes* would be given—at the originative moment, as well as at any given point in space and time.

The nature of cosmic existence, however, is opaque or cloudy at best. Such a non-divine *yes*-sayer—who would be invited to be on a redemptive mission in this world—once conceived in space and time would not necessarily be aware that he or she had agreed to this momentous willingness to be subjected innocently to the external *consequences* of original sin.

Any such creature would have been immaculately conceived and yet would suffer like the rest of earthly humanity—though not from any personal sin. This chosen servant already would have been confirmed in grace by his or her supreme *yes*—a personal, free, and fundamentally full affirmation *given to* God at the moment of being created *out of nothing*. Only the *glory* of that interpersonal union would be "delayed."

If free creatures are *subject to injustice* from the beginning of life on earth there is only one other possibility. In all freedom, their *unwillingness* to give a full response to their Creator *created* that initial injustice itself and hence the necessity to suffer. Such free creatures (each one of us) would be freely at fault in this *originative* sin. They would be deservedly subject to what is known as *original* sin and its consequences. *Only by personal suffering and by the redemptive grace of God would they be able to realize that they are really sinners far more profoundly in need of repentance than at first appears.*

Who of us can affirm that we are wholeheartedly lovers of God and of God's will? Who of us can deny that we are at heart inclined, at least somewhat, toward sin? And should we admit to being sin-conditioned, we can readily acknowledge our real predicament. We can be sure that we are not here in this world as the result of our personal, innocently-made, super-generous decision to help with the redemption of our unjust brothers and sisters.

In the present world, believers in God are not inclined to regard themselves as free of any personal imperfection at the core of their existence. They somehow sense the awesome, personal openness toward sin, especially if temptations and adversities become severe. Even if, in this world, their commissions of sins and omissions of virtue are apparently light, they cannot be sure about the results in some future testing of their resolve.

The prophet David touches on this aspect of our human condition, while mourning his own sins in this life. He not only repents for serious wrongdoing in space and time, but also moans aloud: "For behold I was conceived in iniquities; and in sins did my mother conceive me" (*Psalms* 50:7).

History in the Making

In any event, if we are not innocent co-redeemers in the midst of this world, then the only other possibility looms. We deserve to be subjected to the "history making" original sin of Adam and Eve. We were destined to be conceived in this world, not by an "arbitrary" will of God, but by the effects of our own decision to make *our own will* at least partially arbitrary.

We are not nearly as innocent as we might like to think. And if sinful inclinations have mysteriously deep roots in the depths of our own self-identity, we can even look expectantly for their cause. A profoundly unconscious repression of original responsibility would not be surprising. Yet God continues to respect our freedom—even the ability to deny the depths of our personal and social origins. We are able ("free") to continue the denial.

Originatively speaking, then, as a freely-willing person, everyone is responsible for his or her own suffering: *both* why the misery is at all (originative sin) *and* how to endure it well. The suffering person here in the world of space and time is *not necessarily responsible* for the *particular, relative* origins of adversity, especially at the hands of intruders or other assailants. But each one is *totally* responsible for misfortune *happening to them at all.*

Jesus once told his followers that there were things they were not ready to hear—things that they could not bear to hear. Even so, he promised that the Spirit would come to teach them (*John* 16:12-13). Apparently, however, he thought his hearers were ready to sustain some searing truths even in his time, such as the destruction of Jerusalem, the reality of hell, and the consequences of a faithless life.

Perhaps there is one, singular truth none of us is ever ready for: *our complicity in the very origin of the evil that is ever threatening to engulf us and others.* Could it be that we are dead set against facing the truth of a personal *originative* sin that caused us to *exist-at-all* in this earthly wake-up world?

Multitudes believe in reincarnation. But that amounts to another popular way to escape from facing our immediate responsibility for an originative sin. Reincarnation denies the intrinsic relation of soul and body—holding that the soul can take on different bodies as time goes on. It flouts the essential integrity of the human being and affords, in principle, a way to think that God has to wait for us to come around. We can have as many lives as we "need" to come to enlightenment and peace. With that attitude, the creature becomes in charge of the timing and effectiveness of his or her own 'salvation.' It constitutes another subtle way of denying our radically personal responsibility for an originative sin and our need for a Savior who is wholly other than we who are seeking salvation.

In any case, the Christian evangelist, Paul, claimed to be speaking from the Spirit of God when he said, "...Eye hath not seen, nor ear heard, neither hath it entered into the heart of man, what things God hath prepared for them that love him" (1 *Corinth.* 2:9). Perhaps that is a reference to the gift of *being* that, at the moment of creation *out of nothing*, we immediately and freely, if partly, refused. Our firm hope is that we will be reconciled in the second and final (earthly) effort—an effort laden with the burden of history and with the final judgment day.

We are now facing the results and the prospective consequences. Jesus was not hesitant to proclaim, "...Unless you shall do penance, you shall all likewise perish" (*Luke* 13:3).

Our very *existence* within this world—our shock of a "lifetime"—should be a wake-up call. Here we are not beginning to *be*, but beginning to be-*come*. Our very being is *coming*: after the crash at creation, coming *back* to itself, struggling *through the consequences of its may-being*. All the while, God respects the gift of our freedom and the freedom of the gift that we *are*.

Chapter 4

The Missing Link

Scientists have been looking for "the missing link." Biologists, paleontologists, and others have collaborated for many years. They have been searching for solid evidence of the supposed transition between non-human and specifically human life. They are seeking the *connection* between animals and humans.

Nonetheless, there is another missing link, far more critical for understanding *who we are*. Something seems to be missing between God's infinitely loving, *perfect activity of creating* and some of the *results* of that activity, including the whole cosmos of matter and motion. How could an infinitely perfect act of creating result in so much imperfection?

Besides, the sin of Adam and Eve happened *after* the creation of the world of space and time. So, how could this one sin have affected the subpersonal world on so grand a scale? Moreover, why do disease, destruction, and death affect the *non*-personal world in which there would seem to be *no possible responsibility* for these imperfections? Once creation occurred, why should even subhuman creatures be affected adversely by specifically *human* disobedience?

If we assume the usual, linear way of viewing things, we will miss something in our understanding of creation and of how far personal freedom extends. Why would the disobedience of Adam and Eve change the structures of animals and plants from being completely benign to being potentially destructive?

Curiously, theologians do not often wonder whether there is a *gap*, let alone a *transition*, between the Creator's infinitely perfect act of creating and the condition of created persons like us. They think and talk as though an infinitely perfect Creator could initially cause to be sheerly "out of nothing" a *good*, but somewhat imperfect, *world* that includes the grossly imperfect world of water, earth, a void, and the loneliness of Adam.

In many Christian contexts, also incredible is the *explanation* of the transmission of original sin. This sin is thought quite properly to be the crime of two persons. Nevertheless, it is also said to be an offense that affects their offspring—even down to the core of each inheritor's individuality.

Apparently, we cannot see—nor do we want to see—the "divine anomaly." How could the Being we call God—infinitely personal, infinitely good and powerful—have *let* billions of *innocent* created persons inherit and suffer the catastrophic sin of two *others*.

After all, from what can a dying toddler repent? Furthermore, if God has prepared an incredibly joyful life for the sinless, where is the proportion? Why is an "innocent child" who survives all the vicissitudes of prenatal and neonatal life headed for an adulthood of good and bad choices, probable accidents and sickness, and certain death? Likewise, what about the millions of children who die before birth?

The invisible glory and the freedom of God, hailed by the theistic religions, contrasts sharply with the fallen grandeur and the inherent opaqueness of the visible world. At an unconscious level, thoughtful people sense that something is missing.

How does the massive dullness of the pre-human cosmos—plants, animals, and the rest, sprinkled with light—result *directly* from the activity of infinite brilliance? Can an essentially imperfect world— the world presented in the first verses of *Genesis*—result *directly* from an infinitely perfect Creator?

When the question is urged on us we might be perplexed.

On the one hand, we are told that God is the supreme being, a perfect Being. However, if we allow ourselves to think about it seriously, an infinitely good and infinitely powerful Creator is not only a "supreme" being—the best of the best, so to speak. God is an *infinitely* perfect being whose infinite power could have created only perfect creatures having perfect *freedom*. That freedom-power would be the perfect *potential* to act freely and fully in likeness to their Creator. Only power that is not infinite could create slightly or greatly imperfect beings: but *not out of nothing.*

On the other hand, we experience the cosmic world as marvelous in its own way. But this world is physically and morally beset with stellar explosions, solar tempests, asteroidal collisions, diseases, violence, criminal behaviors, deceptions, and death—a smorgasbord of evils.

The heavenly world, containing only perfect love, harmony, and ecstasy, interfaces with the earthly world of massive indifference, structural weakness, and ultimate failure. Between the two worlds, there is a super-astounding chasm.

Still, let us suppose that the suggested characterization is true: that we were initially gifted with perfect individual freedom and that we personally sinned originatively. Then, *we are the ones who caused that great gulf—the creation gap.* We are the missing link. You and I—not only Adam and Eve—are among God's created persons who profoundly damaged and numbed their own being. Collectively, we must have caused every single aspect of the world's passivity and inertness. The world of matter *as well as the human spirit* is rather opaque *on account of us.* With our originative freedom-power, we "made a mess": the "cosmess."

Our Spiritual Repression

We do not remember deforming and paralyzing ourselves by our first free act. But that could be because we have repressed it so deeply. This *first* act of freedom—an act that was self-abusive—was the very *cause* of the *existence* of repression—spiritual, psychic, and physical. By the dynamics of such universal repression, we are now avidly inclined to blame evil spirits, if not God, for our *original vulnerability* to evil happenings.

We do not let ourselves realize that God *could* not let evil happen *originatively* to any created person. Only those who failed to receive fully the gift of their being would deserve—by their failure—this vulnerability toward attack by malevolent persons: by demons and fellow humans.

The divine prevention of unjust attack would hold only one kind of exception. The Redeemer Himself, or anyone charged to assist in the redemptive act *itself*, would have to be susceptible to injustice "without cause." This person would suffer unjustly as a critical part of the redemptive action. In such a case, however, God would have elicited *full permission* from the person or persons involved.

Disasters like the Holocaust, terrorist attacks, and the multitudes of killer tornadoes, hurricanes, tsunamis, and volcanoes throughout the world elicit the plaintive cry, "How could God let *this* happen?" Such a complaint is most reasonable, except for one thing: ignorance of the *creation gap* and of the missing link.

At the non-temporal moment of our creation "out of nothing," no one could have tempted us. We were gifted to be, whole and entire, face-to-Face with the *Being* of God, though not the glory. We were not subject to temptation any more than Lucifer was. *All* persons must have given pristine individual responses to the gift of their being: full consent, partial consent, or—as did Lucifer and countless angels—no consent at all. The glory of God would suffuse only to those giving full consent.

The idea that God *originatively* allowed the temptation of any perfectly created person is faulty, and constitutes one of the latent, insidious ways we unconsciously cover up the *originative* sin. To the contrary, we can be sure that each created person must have been gifted with complete personal freedom to *be* and to be *self*, without distraction by temptation or anything else. But we botched our being and have buried alive that initial, supremely free and personal, act of *partial* commitment to being.

The genuinely free, *partially* negative consent given by you and me to that originative creation *caused* our (subsequent) vulnerability to overtures and deeds by evil spirits. These spirits had given, in all genuine freedom, their *entirely* negative dissent. ("I will not serve.") They "naturally" then turn to us and "pile on."

Our life is now one of awakening recovery. We are massively subject to all of the after-effects of our personally originative sin—including especially a vulnerability to the forces of evil.

In creation *ex nihilo*, our beings were *purely active* as they were gifted. Even so, by our originative response—our *signature* sin—we must have *cramped ourselves* right within the activity of receiving imperfectly. By our *maybe* kind of receiving, we have *passivized ourselves.*

Such a pre-cosmic "big bang" would have turned at least some of our originatively perfect human *actuality* into *fractuality,* a turbulent *energy* ("dark energy"?). This passive-reactive potential known as energy was *passive* due to the *no* in our *maybe.* Yet, it was *reactive* because of the *yes.* Out of such *ambivalence of being,* now known as *energy, part* of God's activity of redeeming fallen persons was to be effected.

At that point, *Genesis,* in its first pages, picks up the story as the "days of creation" and so much more. In and through spatiotemporal processes, the redemptive activity of God was engaged in recovering our self-fragmented human actuality.

In fact, we seem unable to "recall" the pristine activity of our own participation in the *self-deforming, super-original explosion of being into becoming.* Even after being conceived in the line of time, we still do not begin to become aware of our first *maybe*-saying.

Our numbness about it does not indicate that it never happened. *A peak non-durational* act *can hardly be subject to something time-based, such as memory.*

The *being-based* act of originative sinning was a *proto*conscious act, immediately and freely responding to the act of creation *out of nothing.* Our present fixation on conditions of space and time blocks us from realizing that we *could* not recall it, since it is not strictly "memorable" or subject to memory. Obviously, memory only begins with the origination of space, time, and the measurements thereof that are indigenous to *defectively functioning* human persons.

At the originative moment, each of us was a purely *active* (finite) ability to respond to God. There was no passivity in this immediate *ability.* Rather, our passivity was created *by our actual response.* We were not angels. We were perfect human persons as gifted by God and were also imperfect human persons as received by ourselves. Both the gifting by God and the receiving by ourselves occurred immediately. These acts were perfectly interpersonal. There was no "gap" of duration between the gifting and receiving activities.

Strictly speaking, we did not really *experience* our response. Yet we *knew* it. This first, supremely free act of our be-ing transcends (the passivity of) experience. By being a premier faltering of our be-ing, this originative act *causes the conditions for experience.* We can know it, but cannot experience or "show it" even to ourselves.

Angels do not have recollection or memory, because they are ever present to what is and they do not belong to space and time in any essential way. When they appear to us here, they assume the visages of space, time, and words, but do so for our sake, not theirs.

In this respect, they are quite like God, who knows in the eternal *now*. Like us, however, they are not themselves eternal. They relate directly and mutually with the eternal being of God. They are finite being inter-playing with infinite being forever.

Because they are timeless, there is nothing for angels to "retain" and thus to "recall." We *fallen humans*, however, are all "strung out in being and in perceiving." We try to drag eternity into *our* sphere instead of seeing how appallingly disparate from our originatively gifted being we have become.

Our inability to *remember* a prime act of self-impairment does not mean that we do not *know* it now. We do know it *unconsciously* or rather *preconsciously*—that is, in our *unconscious spiritual* life. Yet we simply fail to *know* it *consciously*.

We can become, however, aware *that* it happened; and we can also know something about what must have been involved. We can know this reality by brutally honest reflection on the partly unconscious (subconscious) questions that haunt our minds.

Even quite conscious questions can be revealing. When confronted by personal tragedies, why is it that so many people ask, "Why me?" This question can be seen as representing the repressive force of our originative sin, of which all our afflictions are symptoms. We say "Why me?" because we do not *want* to know that *we* are the prime, though not by any stretch the exclusive, *cause* of *all* our adversities.

The Power of Repression

In the 19th and 20th centuries, we became increasingly aware of the ordinary human ability for unconscious denial. (We deny but we do not know we are doing it.) One does not have to be a psychoanalyst to detect it. Ordinary folks can see how family members and friends sometimes deny important features of things that they are actually looking at.

Many people can look straight into the bad consequences of their actions and not see them. For instance, they fail to acknowledge how their own youthful misbehaviors have badly impacted their children. Some can also overlook entirely the origin of their actions, as when shoplifters "forget" their first deliberate acts of theft.

So, it is hardly futile to speculate on whether the phenomenon of repression, common in everyday life, has a source in our *spiritual unconscious, right* at the root of our being. And if so, then this *self-hidden, ill-received reality* will be far more decisive and influential in our daily lives than anything stemming from the merely *psychic unconscious.*

After all, theists are ready to believe that God's ways are not our ways, but that our ways are supposed to be quite like God's ways. They have yet to confront, however, the prospect of there being a *spiritual* unconscious.

Within each fallen person's God-like self, the spiritual power of the unconscious is super-real. But this self-hidden power is not like the emotional unconscious. Rather, the emotional or psychic power of the unconscious, with repressive capability, is like the spiritual unconscious, the power that ultimately moves the psychic and the physical.

Helen, the divorced mother mentioned earlier, happens to be an exceptionally caring woman. She admits guilt, however, for some of her decisions in everyday life. That acknowledgement comes largely from her faithful spirit. Sensitive believers who are compassionate and conscientious with others are likely to be most ready *eventually* to recognize something deeper about themselves *and about everyone else in this world.*

At times, we can know and accept how uncaring and unthinking we have been. Such a realization could lead us to suspect that we are now suffering from a chronic and self-distorting affliction.

This condition would be deeper than how we *feel* or want to *feel*. It would entail simply what we *mean* and what we *fail to mean*. Such unconscious denial would be massively greater than any repressive activity exercised about matters of the space-time world.

Truth-twisting, self-aggrandizing activities, such as our common rationalizations for present behavior, could have *originated* only in the most intimate, *timeless* moment of our origins. Our present transgressions, from the slightest to the greatest, could be mainly seen as *symptom-sins* relative to that originative sin within the center of our self.

Of course, in the world of ordinary choices, we are not responsible directly and in detail for *all* the results of our actions. Many other people are involved. We find both the good and the bad coming to us in proportions that seem more or less than we are due.

If we did sin, however, at the prime moment of origins, we thereby *deprived ourselves* of the "paradise" of perfect human nature and the grace of God. So, we can hardly blame *anyone but ourselves* for whatever evil might even accidentally or incidentally result. By freely saying *maybe*, even as God said *be*, we refused to receive and affirm *fully* our finiteness in the face of the infinite.

That free refusal would have plunged us into this *self-caused* "grab bag" of human adversity called the cosmos. With the other fallen humans, we would have *occasioned* the very existence of this region of universal vulnerability. We would have then "naturally" repressed our involvement itself. So, by freely willing to be "pro-choice on *being*," we *caused ourselves* to be *missing* persons.

The Psychological Comes from the Spiritual

Psychological repression is at least a partly *unconscious* denial of painful feelings and events. A man, for instance, denies that he feels bad about being rebuffed by a woman he likes. A woman fails to admit her disappointment in not obtaining a raise in salary. Such emotional phenomena commonly occur in this life.

Would it not be reasonable, then, to wonder whether there is such a thing as *spiritual* repression: an unconscious denial of a super-painful, self-caused act in our immediate relationship with God, in full freedom, as we came into *being*?

If we can psychologically repress, we can also—and even more so—spiritually repress. Instances of repressing *emotion* could be mainly the symptoms of repressing *volition*. At the moment of being created "out of nothing," we could have repressed a perfectly free *act of only partly responsive will.*

At that moment, we were perfectly free to say *fully yes* to the gift and thereby to enter immediately everlasting bliss. But our initial willingness to withhold full affirmation created evil in our *selves*. This passivized condition quite "naturally" caused us now to have to know *and experience* evil as evil—physically, emotionally, morally, spiritually.

Consequently, in the confines of cosmic energy, we find ourselves struggling to recover. The energy is *both* self-imprisoning *and* self-releasing. Such is the profound consequence of our ambivalence in *originatively* saying both *no* and *yes*. The *no* was self-constricting; the *yes* was God-affirming.

If that is the case, our primal defective act of willing can be said to have caused nothing but a beingful havoc. By our structure-altering sin, we created passivity and impotence in both spirit and matter. We thereby created for ourselves the world of good-and-evil. In *this* world, the good ministers to our redemption and the evil is the reason that the redemption is necessary.

At the moment of creation—*ex nihilo*, "out of nothing"—we must have ruptured our *being*. (Our being was not physical at that point. But the self-splitting act caused myriad forms of disjointed, passive parts—including passive materiality itself.) Part of original actuality became somewhat of a fractuality. "Later," our fragmented beings were conceived in the physical world. Then our being-conceived was part of a creation by God *ex aliquo*: "out of something."

The being-in-the-world of Adam and Eve was created in Eden "out of something." So too, our own being-in-the-world was also created in time "out of something": out of the same fractuality as theirs—energy from our originative sin. We thereby entered into the redemptive power of the world's goodness as well as into the testing power of its evil.

We were conceived in this world by the ongoing activity of God's redemptive creation. Once our spatiotemporal conception occurred, our originatively sinful beings were able to grow and to become at least dimly aware of the enormity of our first sin.

Unlike Satan and his angels, we are able to say we are sorry and to seek wholeness from the infinitely loving and forgiving God. The story of Steven's need for making restitution could then symbolize the challenge facing us.

We still might think that creation could not even occur without the production of some evil for creatures to choose or reject. This way of thinking, however, only reinforces our participation in the wiles of the serpent of Eden.

Contrary to the satanic lie in the Garden, God did not want us to know—to have the *experience of*—"good and evil," symbolized by the Tree of that name. Attaining such knowledge would mean that our inceptive choice—our absolutely first choice—was to want to be our own source of truth in what is good and evil. Acting on this attitude would be stupendously evil for us. We would then become structurally inclined to judge how good things *are* by how they *feel to us*—or are *experienced* by us—rather than by how they really *are*.

There is an old maxim that says "experience is the best teacher." However, it only applies "after the fact" of originative sin. Even then one's experiences must be interpreted properly or they merely reinforce false perspectives. According to another saying, "There is no fool like an old fool." Of itself, experience "teaches" nothing. Most telling is *what* we come to *know*—whether in and through *ex-*perience or apart from it. We can teach ourselves, or refuse to teach ourselves, through experience.

In any event, our *fixation* on experiencing things is part of *what resulted*. The question of *how* it happened—how we could have made a bad first act of willing—is not the point here. The first issue constitutes not *how* but *whether*. Speculations about how and why are interesting. Yet, they are rather fruitless until we first know *that* we did it. Only gradually, by convergence of the theological and philosophical evidence, could most of us come to acknowledge our sin *consciously*.

By being reluctant to receive who we are, we distorted the perfect finite freedom God gave us. We *thereby* created evil for ourselves and caused our immensely passive existence. This result yielded for us the deceptive option of being able to act merely on how we feel or "experience."

We said, in effect, *maybe* to the same thing at the same moment. The same originative moment. We contradicted ourselves—our very being—without admitting it. We did not say *yes* to one aspect and *no* to another; we said both *yes* and *no* to the same aspect, namely, our whole being. That is the only way our *first* act of freedom could have occurred: full and perfect as gifted. But, in our case, partial and imperfect as received or exercised.

This originative *reluctance to be freely who we are* might have varied for each of us. In their *maybe*-saying, some might have given an almost full *yes*; others, an almost full *no*. Multitudes of others might have given a largely mixed response.

These degrees of *maybe*-saying would have their consequences in life on earth and, perhaps, in a duration of purgation after death. Yet, none of us in this inherently challenging world would ever be able to judge accurately whose originative *maybe* was where on the *yes-no* continuum. Nor could we ever judge *how much* evil we ourselves originally caused by that first personal *maybe*.

Trying to evaluate which souls happen to be closer to God based on *observed* good or bad conditions and behavior would be futile. There can be no *one-to-one* correlation between a person's actions, or even attitudes, exhibited in *this* world and his or her originative response to creation "out of nothing."

The beingful situation is supremely complex. There is a continuum within each person. Activity from one's spiritual depths reaches right into the moral, mental, emotional, and physical dimensions. There are so many quirks and sidetracks possible in all of these dimensions that such an attempted assessment would amount to folly. A dying Hindu in the arms of Mother Teresa might be holier than that great missionary woman of faith. Who of us has privileged access to the sacred precincts of the individual personhood?

Our frame of reference is much too narrow now. What is critical is how willing we are to appeal to the *unlimited* mercy of God.

Defending Our Repression

When we are fixed on blaming others for the ultimate origin of our miseries, we make it difficult to be sincerely open to God's mercy. The spiritual quagmire of the blame chain goes back to Adam and Eve. We are caught in it because we do not recognize how readily and profoundly we are able to repress.

We are able to deny that we know something because we do not *let* ourselves be conscious of the knowledge. We incline, therefore, to say that we have *no conscious knowledge* of our having given any actual, *immediate* response to the gift of our own being. Therefore, we assume that we never had any opportunity to make a response like that. A clever conceit of thinking: "me no see, it no be."

In addition, it does not even occur that we *might* have responded to God immediately. We simply fault Adam and Eve directly, and God indirectly—largely unconsciously—for allowing original evil to afflict us without our involvement. We hold to our linear fix on space and time as our sole meaningful framework.

Of course, since it is more than unseemly to blame God expressly, most believers would deny that they are really blaming God at all. Another instance of repression, while the rationalizations grow.

A classic way to fault God—unconsciously—is to think that God had to allow evil to exist in order to give us the opportunity to choose the good over the evil. Most believers in the East and the West do not seem to realize that the infinite freedom and perfection of God would necessarily create us as perfectly receptive persons. (*Not* perfectly *receiving*, but perfectly *receptive*.)

At the moment of creation, we *could* have *freely and fully* said *yes* to God's goodness—and to our own. There was no choice between pre-established alternatives; just the potential for pure good *willing*, with the ability to fulfill or fail. With a perfect act of good will, we would have immediately entered ecstatic union with God forever.

Creating us "out of nothing"—with no pre-existing reality—means that God creates only good and perfect beings. God does not create evil *so that* we could choose good by recognizing good as opposed to evil. Nor does God *permit* evil, as many would seem to think.

In creating free persons, God *allows* the evil they choose, but does not permit it. Strictly speaking, permission would mean that God could stop evil-doing, but does not do so for some extraordinary reason. Giving permission would mean positively supporting the evil intention or deed. We recognize this when someone is issued a permit to do something that should not occur in the ordinary course of things. But there is nothing *permissible* about the slightest intent to do or be evil.

A better way to assess it would be that God *initially* creates only perfection. God gave to all created persons the being-power and the doing-power that was necessarily free. From their very origin, these creatures received the perfect executive power to determine their destiny. God, therefore, could not "override God" by giving them *permission* to institute evil. In so doing, God would not be God.

Unlimited power makes it possible and unlimited goodness makes it necessary that God create only beings that are perfectly good and perfectly free. These creatures would be immediately persons in the full sense. They would *be* and be blessed with the full opportunity to say exclusively *yes* to the goodness of being. There would be only the mere *possibility* of saying *no* or *maybe*—that is, of *causing evil*. Only if the creature says *no* or *maybe* would any *actual evil exist* for that creature. This evil would be created *out of* the creature's own gifted finite being *by* that *no*-saying or *maybe*-saying itself.

God infinitely invited us to say *yes*. There was no invitation to say *no* or *maybe*. But since we are finite beings with limited, yet perfect, freedom, we were *able* to say *no* or *maybe* to God's infinitely loving invitation.

Real evil comes into creation *only* through the actual violation of a totally good creature—*by that creature himself or herself.* As it is now, our deepest choices are made between real good and real evil, already existing. That is only because we have already said *maybe* to God and to our entirely good, created being—at the moment of creation from nothing. By the inexorably causal force of *maybe*—

part affirmation, part negation—we set ourselves up for the conflict between good and evil.

By our first act of freedom, now repressed, *we* are the ones who brought into our lives evil as a reality that we are constantly trying to avoid. We now consciously know what is good *as an alternative to* existing evil. We seem to be blocked, however, from considering how we could just as well have known, at the start, what is good as good, without ever knowing evil as an experienced reality.

God *cannot* "experience evil." God *knows* both good and evil. But God *as God cannot* know evil through personal *experience* of its self-destructuring effects. Nor do any created persons who did not sin—whether angels or humans—ever know evil experientially. (Christians believe that, for redemptive purposes, there are, at least, one or two exceptions. And, of course, God as incarnate redeemer experiences the effects of evil, but not sin as sinner.)

In order to be God-like, one does not *have to* undergo *any* struggle or contention with evil. All created persons whose first, supreme act of freedom was fully positive and God-unitive are "confirmed in grace"—that is, confirmed in God. Their total *yes* yields sheer joy, without "experience."

What it is like to act and yet to be without experience is difficult to fathom now, because by our sin we are sated with "experiences." We cannot imagine the life of knowing, loving, and being that is ecstatically joyful, and without any experience—the life of purely trans-experiential, interpersonal union.

We *maybe*-sayers virtually or actually refuse to admit that, at the supremely free moment of being personally created, *we* must have balked. We declined to receive freely—fully and proportionately within ourselves—our own finite being in the *presence* of infinite being, the God of infinite goodness.

Still, there is no such thing as "infinite distance" between God and creature. Infinite difference, yes. The notion of "distance," however, between beings and their Creator comes from the now-largely-unconscious *distancing* that we fallen creatures have done and are doing. And *that* distancing, of course, can only be finite, no matter how "extensive."

We are quite inclined to overlook how God's unlimited power is the power to love unlimitedly. This power is natural to God, though supernatural to us. Our power to love will always be finite, but it does not impair God's originally intended union with us: a marriage of Being-with-being, of the infinite with the finite.

If it is true that we are personally responsible for the origin of evil that affects us, then this admission necessarily follows: any apparent "withdrawal on the part of God" is really our own withdrawal *from* God. We willingly project onto God that for which we ourselves cannot or will not take responsibility—our own primal recession.

We must have *spiritually repressed* our free original withdrawal—our originative action of alienation from God. By making such an admission, we would *find* the missing link.

Chapter 5

The Tree of Adam and Eve

"Who me, responsible for the very *origin* of evil in my life?"

We are not accustomed even to suspecting personal involvement. We have accepted the story of the beginning of evil, as related in *Genesis*. But we have taken it largely at face value.

The common interpretation seems to assert that we exist in this world of problematic choices because we are children of Adam and Eve. Their choice to eat forbidden fruit created a climate of constant choosing between good and evil, life and death—rather than, say, between good and good, life and life.

The new supposition and perspective concerning our responsibility is essentially more personal and central. By the new orientation, we begin to realize that, *in our very beginning* to *be,* we were *both* "face to Face" with God *and* "shoulder to shoulder" with Adam and Eve.

The new vision also calls for meaning that is more holistic for our plight here in the world of space and time. The tree in the middle of the Garden of Eden now lives and grows throughout the structure of our personal and social lives. We are living out the consequences of choosing to "consume the fruit" of the tree of the knowledge of good and evil.

The tree now lives within us. In effect, we chose to be consumers, along with Adam and Eve. A common Christian sentiment even holds that '*In* Adam all have sinned.' Paul, the evangelist, claims that "In Adam, all die" (1 *Corinth.* 15:22). But one might be excused for, at least, wondering whether all have sinned first by sinning *with* Adam in some primal way.

The Tree within Us

Our participation in the tree of the knowledge of good and evil can be seen to involve three parts: branches, trunk, and roots. Each of these three components of a tree is like our now-fallen freedom.

Considering all of the fallen human community, each component represents a special gradation of willing. The *branches* are like the everyday choices of people living their earthly lives. The *trunk* is like the original choice of Adam and Eve, the common point of unity that *initiates, here in space and time* (overtly), the redemptive process. And the *roots* resemble the originative, not-fully-receptive acts of all *maybe*-sayers—their primal acts of unique, individual willing. These root-acts were done "underground." They are now in the domain of our spiritually unconscious lives. Actually, therein they caused the need for the ground under which they rest.

When we start to view a physical tree at a distance, the first thing we might observe is a clump of branches and leaves. Then, coming closer, we would distinguish the trunk from these offshoots. Finally, quite close, we might begin digging around the base of the trunk to lay open some of the roots.

Similarly, attending to the "tree" of choice, we first experience the multitude of our daily decisions. We choose not only about what we do. We also make choices about how we will do it. And we choose the attitude. By that attitude we will receive both the good and bad consequences of our own and other people's decisions. We enjoy life here, but still we suffer evils coming from nature's forces, as well as from wrong turns in human freedom caused by us and by others.

We also see that our ordinary experiences and choices are like branches stemming from a trunk. The experiences and choices of our predecessors condition them, all the way back to the original sin of Adam and Eve as the "trunk choice." That "original choice" *confirmed* the originative will or choice of our first parents (their primal *maybe*). And it got them fully and directly involved with good-and-evil.

This first behavioral decision, popularly known as original sin, is the stem or trunk from which all of our everyday choices serve as branches. Theological or religious interpretations of this wrong turn in freedom attempt to respond, among other questions, to our most painful complaints. "Why *me*? Why am *I* hurting?"

Usually, however, these reflections go no further than the "trunk of the tree." With this catastrophic disobedience of Adam and Eve the mystery of our *history* began. Still, the "tree of our involvement in good and evil" must have roots as well.

The branches and the trunk of a tree are visible above the ground. Similarly, both ordinary sins and original sin have become evident to our conscious minds. We often consciously experience the sins of ourselves and of others and especially of the many effects. And we consciously believe that we are affected by parents who had parents all the way back to the beginning of human history.

But history itself, as a whole, has *roots* that feed it from below its surface. Things within the conscious mind have feeders from the unconscious. If we are going to know something about these feeder-roots, we will have to listen carefully in faith. We will also need sensitively to exercise intuition and reasoning in order to dig for deeper evidence of *why* we suffer.

The Inside Story of Eden

The branches of a tree are many, and so are the roots. Only the trunk is one. Similarly, the "trunk sin"—the original sin of Adam and Eve, of one couple—could stem from the primal or "root sins" of *each* and *all* of us, including Adam and Eve themselves. "Root sins" form solidarity with the first couple's sin in Eden. They come together forming a trunk.

Each of us, at the moment of our creation "out of nothing," must have received somewhat weakly the gift of being. Thereby we were destined eventually to come into the cosmos, as we are, in grave need both of redemption and of recovery through the struggles of generation, education, and sanctification.

If God is infinitely perfect, then each individual has been given his or her own opportunity to proclaim fully *yes* to the gift of being. Whatever the response, the created person would be given a share in the destiny of persons who decided similarly. In this way, those who said *maybe* naturally formed a corporate state of sin and redemption, headed by Adam and Eve as the chosen progenitors.

We need to realize the missing link. We ought to acknowledge that infinite beneficence must have gifted each one of us with complete power to be perfectly good and free at the moment of creation "out of nothing." But between God's infinite holiness and the desperate condition of our now-cosmic existence there is one factor missing. This "missing link" must be our immediate distrust and imperfect reception of the gift of being-at-all at the moment of creation. This gap was created well "before" Adam met Eve in the Garden. (We might keep in mind that we say "was," even though we know that this act of creation—as it transcends time—was not temporal and could also be referred to in the present tense.)

How the missing factor came about might be interpreted variously.

One storyline could go like this. Among all those who said the originative and supreme *maybe*, Adam and Eve were the "leaders" by their particular boldness of being and willing. They could have been outstanding in their manner of saying *maybe*.

With the rest of us, Adam and Eve were human persons created *out of nothing*. Along with us, they gave their first, free, individual responses: *maybe*. Immediately, their beings, like ours, suffered a collapse.

Immediately also, God apparently selected them to "be first" at trying to be awakened to their initiating sin. They were chosen to represent the now-unconscious plight of all of us *maybe*-sayers, who had put ourselves commonly into a comatose condition of being.

God would then have fashioned these two leaders into redemptive form, including functional matter (bodies). They were put on trial in Eden in order to reveal *to themselves, and eventually to all of us,* how truly weak and faithless all *maybe*-sayers really are.

God, therefore, created them *out of something* (dust, a rib). This creation was really a "re-creation" or the initiation of *recovery.* "In time," by being conceived in the cosmos, all *maybe*-sayers might thereby experience the consequences of their originatively rendered goodness and badness before God.

But what was the original something (the "dust") from which the Creator fashioned Adam? It could plausibly have been the elements of passive-reactive (redemptive) matter and energy that would have burst out from the primary break in our being. All of us *maybe-sayers* would have caused, immediately and together, this rupture and its consequences: at the non-durational moment of receiving our pure creation *out of nothing*. (In contemporary physics, for instance, concepts like "dark matter" and "dark energy" might amount to secondary analogues of this *primary energy* analog that followed from our faltering receptivity in the first creation.)

In the Garden, then, Adam and Eve, standing for all of us, were given a test. And they failed. Indeed, God had spoken as though their fall was a foregone conclusion: "Of every tree of paradise thou shalt eat: but of the tree of knowledge of good and evil, thou shalt not eat. For in what day soever thou shalt eat of it, thou shalt die the death" (*Genesis* 2:16-17).

Their original sin done in Eden is believed to have initiated human history in this temporal world of good and evil. Whether the story of Eden is taken literally or symbolically or as partially both, Adam and Eve fell and started the history of their *ex-istence*. They initiated in space and time, for themselves and their offspring, a *struggling way of being* that was to be terminated, sooner or later, by death and *final* judgment.

We could be conceived, then, in their *original* sin because we had originatively predisposed ourselves for this inheritance. But if we had not—if we had said fully *yes*—we would have entered freely and naturally into the immediate union with God at the moment of creation. Or, by saying fully *no,* we would have plunged into hell.

By our own rudimental reluctance, we fell from the opportunity to unite fully with eternity. That fall contributed to the very existence of space and time—*space* being a kind of fallen-away receptivity (a passive receptacle) and *time* being a kind of fallen-away attempt to recover gradually our full receptivity.

Hence, with multitudes of others so afflicted, we had to be brought into, and through, the processes of space and time. The specific means for this recovery included human generation, headed by Adam and Eve and their "history-making" fall. (Even were it so that, as Jewish and Islamic people believe, we did not inherit Adam's sin, we nonetheless "inherited" the results—a *maybe* world that includes struggle and frustration.)

In the Christian Testament, Paul said, "Wherefore as *by one man* sin entered into this world, and by sin death; and so death passed upon all men, in whom all have sinned" (*Romans* 5:12). Sin entering the world is not necessarily the same as all human beings sinning. But, for all those humans who *did commit* sin originatively, doing their sinning is a critical reason *why* they *had* to enter this world, wherein Adam was the functioning head.

We might ask ourselves a most serious question. Did we somehow make a supremely original "choice"—a *protoconscious* act of will? That act of will would now be buried deep within our preconscious life—our *spiritually* unconscious life, not simply our emotionally unconscious life. That decisive act of will would have been whether to receive, fully or not, the gift of our being.

Would this preeminent decision feed into the events of Adam and Eve, like subconscious roots leading into a trunk above the surface of our minds? Is there, then, a repressed choice—a *root* choice—in the deep, dark ground of the suffering human soul that answers the question: why am I hurting?

God let us suffer the consequences of our first parents' fall and the "human condition"—really the *fallen* human condition. By doing so, was not God then simply respecting the dignity of our freedom and the consequences of our originative "choice"—our primal willing—at the moment we were created out of nothing?

The Roots of *Maybe*

Speculating about what happened at the instant of our originative creation could be interesting. But, one thing is certain. This truth is insuperable: if God is truly infinite in *both* power *and* goodness, we had to have been created in *perfect* freedom by an *infinitely* loving God. That creation could not have happened by evolution wherein the less imperfect comes gradually out of the more imperfect. Nor could it come via "creationism" wherein the less-than-perfect kinds of creature are seen to come immediately and directly by act of the infinitely perfect Creator.

So, what does it mean to say *maybe*? We can surmise that *maybe*-sayers might have freely "said," in one way or another—intuitively, freely, and instantaneously—"What's this? What would it be like to *be* God, not just to be *like* God?" Or "I don't know what it means for me to be simply finite; it must be great to be infinite." Alternatively, "Wouldn't it be better for me to be a creator and not just a creature?" Or something else that was similarly self-centered, half-hearted, and indecisive.

We were *able* to be totally God-centered right from the start. But we were also *able* to be self-centric rather than God-centric. Self-centrism as a condition of being was not an "evil alternative" to be chosen in opposition to "the good alternative," the total love of God. There were no "alternatives" called "good and evil." This "chosen" or willed self-centric condition was a *possibility—a possibility of our creative being*. We created this self-centrism *out of something*: out of the perfect finite freedom with which we were immediately gifted. We thereby set ourselves up for good and bad choices as a consequence.

Indeed, our creation of an initial self-centrism would have *caused* the floundering kind of symptomatic egocentrism found in us today. Deep in the heart of our *being*, we *maybe*-sayers would have planted our own "tree of choice," now most profoundly buried in the lost Eden within us.

No-sayers, on the contrary, would say, "I want to *be* God, *not* merely be *like* God." Or "I do not *will* to be finite; I *will* to be infinite." Their free willing would be made without any immediate shadow of reluctance, with no "ifs," "buts," or "maybes" about it.

By their own ability for free activity, they would have obliterated their "freedom of choice." They would have left themselves totally bent on hating their Creator, as well as themselves and others. No choice would then remain, just the "satisfaction" of hating from the depths. Hell is forever.

Full *yes*-sayers would say freely and definitely *yes* to the gift of being and the infinite goodness of God. Right from the moment of creation "out of nothing," these full-affirmers of the Creator and of creation would exercise perfectly their freedom to love God and all others, including themselves. There would, of course, be no "garden experience" through the mediation of Adam and Eve. Immediately, directly, *within* eternity, they would be *affirming* God forever.

But we, by saying *maybe* to God, would have created our "tree of the knowledge of good and evil" right from its roots. We would have freely placed reservations on the unconditional love that God showed in giving us our being at the moment of creation—a moment now unconscious and repressed.

We must have *semi-passivized ourselves*. We freely established a somewhat selfish being as opposed to purely self-giving being. The structure of our whole being was flattened out, so to say, in order to accommodate our partial self-debasement.

Originally, we were destined to be *purely active* receivers of union with God. Instead, we suffer enduringly from our passivity and self-constriction. Even now, change toward betterment is rather blocked or slowed by our reactive-passivity.

But, if we progress, however haltingly, that is only because we can see the self-blighted condition for what it is. And we can humbly acknowledge the need for the Savior of our whole being. Passive (cosmic) matter itself then serves *both* as the ground that buries the primary sin away from our awareness *and* as the soil of our potential repentance.

We are still left wondering why, at the very moment of originative creation—without anyone tempting us—we would freely hesitate to affirm fully God's goodness. Christians, however, might learn to pose a similar question about Lucifer and the outright God-denying angels. How could they *do* such a thing? And who tempted *them*?

We might ask, even from the usual, time-fixed perspective, "Who tempted Lucifer?" And we thereby see that no one could have done so. Only passivized persons *like we are now* could be *susceptible* to temptation. And we could be tempted only *after* we had said *maybe* on our own, *untemptedly*.

Nor could Lucifer or anyone else have tempted us when we began to be at the *very* beginning—the beginning of beginnings. We were, at that moment, acting uniquely. We were doing our first immediate activity of giving free *interpersonal* response to our infinitely loving

Creator—*free of even the slightest tug of temptation.* Free to be fully *with* God.

Passive Potency Contains our Temptability

In order to understand an *untempted* act of sheer freedom and to appreciate our involvement within the classic *human predicament*, a basic examination of the traditional ideas of *act* and *potency* will be helpful. *Act* and *potency* are concepts first derived from a common sense analysis of everyday reality.

The word *act* is the dynamic word that comes from Aristotle's deeply rooted analysis of ordinary being. Yet it can receive a deeper, existential meaning—meaning that was not, in effect, available to that pre-Christian thinker. Attending to our "-ing" words can give us leverage.

A tree, for instance, can be seen in its *secondary acts* of greening, growing, leafing, and the like. But it can also be seen as dynamically *treeing*—being-this-kind-of-*being*, as different from being a squirrel or a cloud or a different kind of tree. The *act* of being this kind of tree has been called the tree's *substantial form*.

Every natural substance is "doing its thing," that is, being-itself, whether this being happens to be tree-ing, bird-ing, human-ing, or whatever. These *substantial acts* are recognizable by any mind that is alert to nature. They are assumed—and not directly treated—by scientists as well as by common sense observers. This tree is *tree*-ing, not just growing and leafing. This bird is fundamentally *bird*-ing, not just flying and chirping. Jane is *human*-ing, not just walking and talking.

There is so much more that is intrinsic to everyday beings. Besides their *acts*, their natures are teeming with potencies. Basically, these potencies come in two quite different kinds: *active* and *passive*.

Even when you are sleeping, you can be said to have the *active* potency to walk. An *active* potency is an *ability* to *do* something. An actual potential, not a theoretical or hypothetical one.

You also have the *passive* potency to be affected by your acts of walking or talking or breathing, and the like—*and as well as by the activities of others acting upon you.* These *passive* potencies are real; but they are *not at all* active potencies—abilities to *do*. *Passive* potency is an ability or capacity *to be done to*—to be done to or to *be determined* this way or that, by yourself and by other entities.

In the cosmos, passive potencies are as real and actual as active potencies; they are real characteristics of substances. A dog has the capacity or passive potency to be affected by or determined by—to some extent—its act of *barking*, and by acts of other natural agents acting upon it in space and time. But it has no passive potency to be *directly* affected by an act of thinking or reading or speaking. And the canine simply has no *active* potency for—that is, capacity for doing—these latter acts.

Passive potencies are poorly receptive potencies that necessarily cause weakened receptivities. They are chiefly known by the active potencies that *constitute* a given kind of substance. By knowing the tree's active potency or ability to produce peaches, we know thereby the passive potency of a peach tree to bear peaches and not apples or anything else—an ability "to be peached," not "appled" or "peared."

When we consider not only physical beings, but spiritual ones, the meanings of act and potency are retained. But they are transformed. Interpersonal activities involve actuality and potentiality of a higher, yet similar interrelationship.

Temptability, of course, is a feature of a spiritual and interpersonal kind. An ability to be tempted is a passive potency—an "ability to be done to." This susceptibility to *be acted upon* or to *be passively determined* by another, and even by oneself, was *not originatively* gifted by God.

God creates purely active finite beings—each one is a person— entirely *capable* of interrelating with all the others in a non-passive, fully-open, relational way. Every such being is an ability to be acted *with,* to be *related to*—not done to or acted upon.

At the absolute moment of being gifted with a perfect finite being (creation *ex nihilo*), our being had no passive potency and was itself a *purely* active potency—a potency to *receive being* perfectly. Since we were without the constraints of any temptation, we *could* have exercised our active potency fully and immediately. We would then have been perfectly happy forever.

At that first moment of being, *both act and active potency* were really *actualities*. The one actuality was the very God-gifted being itself. The other was that very being's *potency* or ability to *receive* itself. In other words, we were able, freely and immediately, to receive the act of being as gifted. The very act of being that we were gifted to be was able to receive itself perfectly or imperfectly.

But, within our originative do-ing, we exercised our purely active potency imperfectly. We immediately refused to receive *fully* our very own being. This self-distorting act of receiving *caused* multiple and massive *passive* potencies to exist in us—under conditions of "lameness." By virtue of these passivities, we were vulnerable and *apt* for being tempted: drawn out of our God-gifted selves to be "shaped" by others. And we were subject to the whole of space and time, to be conceived and to labor in existence, to become diseased, and to die.

The answer, then, to our question about why we would hesitate revolves around the gift we were given. We were given the ability to be *purely* like God. Not *impurely* like God. Freely God-like. As God *is* God's infinite *Be*-ing, we *are* our finite *be*-ing.

Each one is a *self*, God-like, with the powers of self-destiny. We can be our self either on our own or *with*-God. Why not *with*-God, instead of without-God? Simply because we *willed* to be our own "boss." We tried to *have* our be-ing, not to *be* it.

In our first act of impartial freedom, two personal beings were *directly* involved: God and self. We freely inclined toward the self more than toward the Other. We then gained some "control" over our own unique being—thereby, however, deceiving *ourselves*. If God were to have prevented *that* from happening, we would hardly be free. God gifts us the freedom to be our own *be*-ing.

Through our *originative* "hesitation in being," we became thereby self-*contaminated*, instead of self-*receptive*; and we "took control" of ourselves by passivizing ourselves—freely responding to *being* in a manner quite unGod-like. We tried to *have* our be-ing, rather than to *be* our *be*-ing. Our resulting acts and activity are freighted with the need for behavior (be-*have*-ment), whether good or bad. We are 'be*having*,' rather than simply *be*-ing.

Resolving Our *Maybe*

From this fundamental failure in self-determining at the roots of our *be-ing*, we suffer immensely. But we also labor under a second level of will: the failure in Eden, at the beginning of fallen human *be-havior*. Their original sin in the Garden should have awakened Adam and Eve to their *originative* sin at the roots of their *be-ing*.

Like the trunk of a tree above the surface of the ground, their Garden choice is detectable and consciously knowable. We can, at least, hear about it and consciously believe in it through Scriptural Revelation.

Additionally, the third level of choice follows from the other two. Once introduced, by Adam and Eve and their progeny, into this *maybe* world of both good and evil, we individuals are constantly choosing. We are making ordinary choices. These are the branches and leaves of the "tree of choice." These ordinary choices *stem from* our primal choice (roots), as well as from Adam and Eve's serpent-tempted original choice (trunk) to "eat the forbidden fruit."

Our ordinary choices—as we interact in everyday situations—are attempts to resolve our supreme *maybe*, our root-choice, into a final *yes* or a final *no*. We are trying to take ourselves out of our *maybe*—a stance both good and evil—into one or the other, *either* good *or* evil. There is no room for even the slightest evil in heaven or for the slightest good in hell.

So, in the midst of our present "*maybe* condition" we are called to assert absolutes—absolutes of morality, beauty, knowledge, and being. By our active efforts, affirming what is good and denying what is evil—by "rising above" our *maybe* condition—we begin to say *yes* to our redemption and salvation. We are trying to move out of *maybe* toward a complete and unreserved *yes*, but only within the saving power and presence of God.

Keeping Adam and Eve in Focus

If this interpretation or a similar version is *basically* true, we are mega-*maybe* creatures struggling in the cosmos. The three levels of human choice—the Primal, Original, and Ordinary—permeate the entire human venture in space and time. Two of these levels are especially personal to us: the Primal and the Ordinary. The other is specifically personal only to our first parents, who "brought us into this world," and who brought this world into us. But it is a world for which we had already set for ourselves by creating, out of our gifted receptivity, our own passivity.

As an inheritance, however, the "original choice" of Adam and Eve in Eden profoundly affects our ordinary choices. Many theists have always believed in the poignantly penetrating effect of this inheritance—or, at least, consequence—of the "history making" sin. But they do not seem to have been aware of how the fall of Adam and Eve *itself* could have been the *effect* of much more subterranean, critical, personal choice on *their* part, as well as on *our* part.

Before we began to be in space and time, we began to *be*. (This "before" is not temporal, but is an ontological or beingful priority.) By bungling our supremely causal choice, at the moment of primal creation, we generated the need for a line of parentage throughout the ages.

But this act of self-determination at the root of our being has been spiritually repressed. We are now *unwilling to know* our original deformation of the gift of perfect freedom. And then, in our resultant highly imperfect freedom, we afford ourselves the "luxury" of not having to admit how purely free we are by *orignative* nature.

Theists are called to acknowledge what is missing between God's infinite goodness as Creator and the gravely self-impaired freedom of *every one of us*, who are profoundly wounded human *persons*. That missing element is not the trunk freedom of Adam and Eve. It is the sin *in our roots*, our principal self-affliction: a sin of *maybe-saying* that is *both* radically personal *and* radically social.

We must have freely failed to fulfill our perfect, purely active, God-gifted *power to will* at the moment of sheer creation. We did not unite fully with our Creator.

By the same act of ill-willing, we must have effectively denied this originative activity of our *be*-ing. Each one's *power* to love (*will*) had the ability *even to repress itself*, as well as to repress its pristine activity of defectively receiving *being*. The ill-willing person can repress—keep unconscious even to oneself—the very power itself of completely and immediately determining received destiny. The very power of *agent will* is unconsciously denied.

Philosophers and theologians will occasionally write of an agent *intellect*—a *purely active* power involved in knowing. But they are virtually silent on anything like an *agent will, its counterpart in loving.*

The purely active power to *love* God, self, and all others, fully and immediately with "our whole heart," must have been repressed by the person's misuse of that power itself. This *agent will* of ours, in effect, yielded itself to passivization by its own active freedom-power. So, the effects *in this life* include the *defective* condition of our will. It is now recognized simply as a *passive potency of our soul* that requires stimulation by outside forces in order to operate—to choose, and to self-direct. Our passive will now substitutes for our originatively-gifted active will.

Later, we will probe both the primal and the ordinary levels of our personal choice. Through dedicated attention to the heart of our minds, we can try to help ourselves realize what we have done to ourselves. We can come to see that by denying consciously any guilt for an original bad "choice" or willing activity, we may be adding to our guilt here within the world of human relationships and ordinary choices. (If it is "by their fruits you shall know them," it is likewise "by their roots will their fruits be affected.")

We may also begin to feel more deeply the mercy of God. We may come to realize *why* God suffers—with us and even within us—in a redemptive and incarnate way, though not in our desperately passive way.

In any event, first let us take a closer look at the story of Adam and Eve. Are there any clues right within their story that might lead us into this deeper dimension of personal responsibility and choice? Can we go digging effectively around the trunk to expose some of the roots?

Chapter 6

The Original Choice

Adam and Eve stand under a tree eating a forbidden fruit. Then, for the first time, they are ashamed to be naked. They make efforts to cover themselves.

Some believers today call the act of consuming the fruit an error. But many retain the traditional view that this infamous "first choice" was an act of defiance. More than a mistake, the *willingness* to do what God solemnly told them not to do had made Adam and Eve sinners. They *deliberately* "missed the mark." They sinned and the consequences followed.

But what about us? Were we conceived and born on planet Earth only to "miss the mark" initially because of someone else? Were we *shoved off* the mark? Did Adam and Eve "make us do it"? Did we inherit quite innocently their sin or, at least, its sinful consequences? These questions and many others deserve our best response.

We can begin by reviewing briefly how Adam and Eve became established in this world of time and space.

Clues in *Genesis*

The *Book of Genesis* says that in the beginning, God created the heavens and the earth. This material world began to be by the power of One who is eternal. But not even the whole created world itself, including the world of spirit, is eternal. It has a beginning: with time or, like the angels, independent of time.

Indeed, the kinds of things and their interrelationships that were created in the world of *passive matter* seem to come to be in stages. By an upward moving hierarchy, they go from the simply physical to the complexly biological to the virtually spiritual.

At first there was a "formless void." This picturesque manner of speaking in *Genesis* could mean that every element of the whole works *ultimately* came "out of nothing." Or, less metaphorically, it could mean that the particular elements of the cosmos, such as light, air, water, plants, birds, and so forth were made from *something*— *ultimately* from a void, if not from chaos.

For instance, *Genesis* reports God's words, "Let there be light." But *how* light came to be is not said; what is said is simply *by whose executive power* it arrived. The various elements of space and time came into existence successively and in a certain order.

Creation "out of nothing" (*ex nihilo*), however, is not a process. It is immediately and fully effective. It is flawless. There is simply the full and perfect gift of unique created persons, given by an infinitely good Creator.

So, in *Genesis* we confront a less than fresh creation: a creation *ex aliquo* ("out of something"). Whether one's interpretation happens to be literal or figurative, God is said to make things gradually, step by step, as it were. Starting from a void, God forms day and night, the earth and stars, the plants and animals, and eventually a man and a woman.

As well as being the supreme Creator of the elements—*ultimately* from nothing—God is a *maker*, who uses pre-existing materials to form new creations. Adam was made from the dust of the earth, and Eve from a rib of Adam.

The basic creation of the material world was done in six "days," most likely meaning six lengths of time, *not necessarily* 24-hour periods. The coming of evening and morning during these days could readily be seen symbolically rather than literally. In any case, taken either literally or figuratively, these six days indicate a process and progression—whether or not the "leaps" from lower to higher forms were lightening fast or massively gradual.

So, on the seventh day, God "rested," possibly suggesting that it took effort, as it were, to craft the whole cosmos. Not that God had to fight hostile spirits, as various pagan stories held, but that the matter of the stages of *this* creation had to be "worked" to conquer its passivity, its active resistance. (It was also a way of telling people to be God-like and to rest on the Sabbath day in their covenant with the Creator.)

Augustine, the classic Christian theologian, seems to have taken God's creating activity to be "immediate" and "simultaneous," and as occurring on "one day." He held, however, that some things were created whole and actual and that others were created as potential and destined to unfold gradually. So, even he saw original creation as involving some imperfection or lack of fulfillment and thus as involving a process.

Despite this special intuition about God and creation, Augustine still seems to miss the full force of the creation *ex nihilo*.

On the one hand, such creation could *only* be of *perfect* persons, effected by the infinitely perfect act of God. These created persons are not "gifted" with *any* passive potency or with processes. They are perfect, purely actual, finite beings.

On the other hand, *subpersonal* beings are necessarily *imperfect*. They were created out of some kind of a *void*—not out of "nothing." A "void" is basically an emptiness within something, perhaps within a fullness. What is the something, the fullness, for this void?

The whole cosmos and its effects could only have been caused by God working on what originatively perfect persons *produced* by *responding imperfectly* to their pristine creation.

Some have taken the *Genesis* story as reporting a vision that was communicated to Moses (or Adam) about the origins of the world, and that it was not a report of physical events necessarily. However, the world that such vision would be *about* can now be seen directly. It is process-ridden and imperfect. Even if the "six days" are strictly methodological, pedagogical devices to make it easier to understand the world's origin, that world still thunders its deficiencies.

In any case, the main point of the two creation accounts in *Genesis* is God's masterful authority and control.

Yet, when we examine the texts, despite particular discrepancies, we find that the relationship of creatures to the Creator is depicted as rather impersonal. Even the life breathed into Adam (in the "second" creation account) is being treated as less than fully personal. God "breathing" on the newly formed, not-yet-alive creature is hardly relating Person-to-person. This act is basically Person-to-thing.

Here we find a clue to something significant about the nature of the cosmic creation. The material creation is not person-centered, but function-centered. It is essentially a means to an end. Its purpose would appear to be the process of redemptive recovery. Certainly, the purpose of this material creation—with its *intrinsic passivity*—is *not simply* for the glory of being.

The making of Adam and Eve is characterized in rather functional terms. Adam comes from the dust of the earth and Eve from the rib of Adam. This activity seems to be continuous with the making of the impersonal forces and factors of the cosmos during the other five days of creation.

Whether the time be regarded as short or long—six days or six billion years—both creationists and evolutionists treat creation as a *process*. The creation goes from stage to stage. All or most of the creatures are seen as coming out of something else—if only out of a void or chaos.

Such a creation is in no way "creation out of nothing" (*ex nihilo*), but "out of something"—out of something that is ready to "be done *to*" or acted *upon*. (God is not a Magician, pulling pure creatures out of, or through, imperfect ones. Or plopping perfect creatures out of nothing into the procession of imperfect ones.) This "creation" or *making* includes a space-time framework, even as does the account of Adam and Eve in Eden before the "fall."

From whatever angle we view it, there is nothing perfect about the creation of passive matter and motion. All things therein—in "the heavens and the earth"—are quite imperfect, despite their amazingly intricate structure and beauty.

Nevertheless, we read that God is pleased with the levels of this creation *ex aliquo* (out of something). Each is declared to be good. God even dialogues with God when determining to create man and woman in divine likeness.

But, at the moment of the making, so to speak, God is not depicted in dialogue with those creatures themselves. God does not directly *speak with them*. There is no *immediate* "God said, we said." *This* creation is noticeably less than an *inter*personal activity.

In the second account (*Genesis* 2), the activity of God is portrayed as more personal than in the first account. God talks to Adam and tells him what is good and bad.

Yet, Adam and Eve in the Garden of Eden were not in heaven. Immediately, there was a question of what they could or could not do. Such a question could not have arisen in heaven, where there would be only supreme light, harmony, fulfillment, and peace.

Of the fruit of all the trees in the Garden, except one, they were permitted to eat. Adam and Eve had a continuing choice of doing good or doing bad. They were obviously living with God on a trial basis.

Their interpersonal relationship with God and with each other was not an union of rapturous bliss. They had the real, ongoing prospect of saying *no*, as well as *yes*. Although they seemed to be on good terms with God, Adam and Eve were far from being continuously and ecstatically intimate with the Divine. Moreover, they were far from being at home with each other. They were conversant, but not contented.

Before they sinned, they were naked and unashamed. Quite naive.

Right after their fall, they were embarrassed to be in front of each other. They also hid from the presence of God, indicating perhaps that they had been unaware of how they looked before their sin.

Their hiding would seem to mean that they were not only ashamed of disobeying God, but also of how untrustworthy they had been in the Garden from the start. Their yielding easily to temptation should have revealed *to them* their initial naiveté about how lacking in intimacy of relationship they were with each other and with God even *before* the sin.

The *functionality* of their bodies—naked or otherwise—meant that they were designed for work, more than for celebration, right from the heart of Eden. After they completely succumbed to the wishes of the tempter, unwanted self-knowledge was brought to light by their sin. They *experienced* both guilt and shame.

But there was a difference between their guilt and their shame.

Guilt involves the awareness of having done something wrong. Remorse about disobedience. Shame, however, is much more than distress over having *acted* wrongly. Shame involves disgrace about being who one is: an unworthiness of *being*, not just of be-*havior*.

Although they did not realize it at the time, Adam and Eve were *dis*-graced even before they made their wrong choice of *action*. And once they disobeyed God's command, their bad choice of behavior triggered their remorseful awareness of *what kind of being* they were: ignoble and temptable.

They alone could have *made themselves* that way: disgraceful while completely denying it even to themselves. Their original sin of *misbehavior* over the fruit of a tree made them confront their own ill will *and* their less than perfect condition of *being*.

The structure of their observable selves, with all their functional bodily parts, especially organs of social generation (their genitals), reveals them to be in desperate need of recovery, individually and communally. Even before the explicit temptation from the evil one under a tree, they were living in a manner quite like the way they existed after the fall. They did not stand *in the Garden* as perfect created persons.

Why were they standing *there*? Why *in a garden*? And why did they require food at all? Why did they need a mouth and the whole complex of internal organs and cells that comprise their spatial and temporal manner of being as individuals?

Were they not created "a little less than the angels"? Not at all as angels, of course. But, as God said *Be*, were they not unencumbered by the weights of space and time, and of *passivity* in their matter?

Surely, Adam, Eve, and all other human persons could have been created as human persons, *but without any passivity in either their matter or their spirit*. Passivity necessarily signifies *the* condition of *imperfection*.

Their *originative* creation "out of nothing" could not possibly have involved *any passive* matter. There was simply *active matter* (pure receptivity of essence) proper to perfect *human* beings. There could have been no bodily—and hence ontologically imperfect—structure to their gifted beings.

Adam and Eve would receive, of course, functional bodies at the moment of their *original* creation out of dust and out of a rib—out of some kind of passivity. (And we would likewise in space and time be created redemptively out of the fragmented condition of *our* originative be-ings.) This beginning "make over" of their thoroughly self-afflicted beings was a necessary part of the prospects for *fallen* human beings to emerge from the repression and the denial of their *originative* response to creation.

Indeed, the portrayal of Adam and Eve as having been created from the dust of the earth and a rib shows their impersonal, non-originative condition. Thereupon, God was working with them in the process of the recovery from the crashed condition that had occurred "well before" the Garden experience of making an "original choice."

Being bodily, with organs, necessarily signifies neediness, despite how well supported by conditions of pleasure and satisfaction. The specific reason for organs is to be a means to an end. While organs can be treated as ends in themselves momentarily by our attitudes, they are in themselves (etymologically) "fleshly tools"—the means to maintain a whole that is greater than themselves. That *whole* is ordered to redemption, far more than to creation.

Even the whole organismic body itself is essentially a means, not an end. The physical body—however "perfect" it might seem—is functioning in every cell for the good of something *other* than that cell itself. And so it was in Eden, even before the fall. *That* is not the condition of perfection, even when the *functioning* is often seen to be "perfect functioning." Perfect *functioning* is not perfect *being*.

People usually think of the human body as a means the soul uses to know physical reality—specifically knowing through the senses. They rarely wonder, however, why the body would be required for the person to know physical things. Why not know physical things in a non-sensory way, something like God and the angels do?

Why not know all of cosmic reality, as a whole and in every part, through spiritual powers alone, in a manner similar—but not at all identical—to the way of the blessed angels? Did God just arbitrarily decree it to be that way, or is there some necessary reason for our functionality to be based in passivity? Death, of course, is a major result of functional passivity.

The sin of Adam and Eve—traditionally called original sin—could have been perhaps *an initial stage in arousing recognition*. This sin could have revealed to them that their spatiotemporal bodies were a sign of an already committed *originative sin*. Right from the start in the Garden, even before succumbing to the serpentine temptation, they might well have been called to recover from a *protoconscious* sin that was, at that point, spiritually unconscious (preconscious).

Their bodies were not evil at all. Their bodies were serving as *part* of the means for their *recovery*, and for the recovery of succeeding generations of fallen human persons—recovery from an *originative* sin. And, of course, their bodies served as sacral signs that evil (originative sin) had been done *by themselves* to their whole *being*. The messenger should not be blamed at all for the negative message. Similarly, our bodies should not be regarded as bad, just because they represent recovery from the originative bad within us.

No *originative* creature of God could have been imperfect, except by *self*-diminishment. Even before their sin with the serpent, Adam and Eve had bodies that consisted of "parts outside of parts." These parts were specifically *means* to the functioning of other parts and of the whole. Having "parts outside of parts" means distension, the condition of being not fully or perfectly integral. Integrity of being is inherently compromised. The whole of the physical body stands as redemptively good, but is not an originative condition of being for anyone.

In *Genesis* we find no specific expression of man and woman being created "out of nothing." How could there be? Such a creation would have been immediately *personal*, and could not have been anything as impersonal and as functionalistic as God blowing breath or constructing one body from part of another.

Creation *ex nihilo* is the *infinitely intimate* act of love that creates the *finite* power to be loving—interpersonally and unconditionally. This primal created power is intended immediately for *celebrational life everlasting*, not for functional temporal survival.

By contrast, the creation stories of *Genesis* are "process stories." They may have symbolic reference to creation *ex nihilo*. They serve mainly, however, as ways to account for the early stages of God's *redemptive and restorative* activity. By attempting to reform crashed creatures into newness of being, God begins to reclaim from self-destructiveness the immensely resistant "human race."

The whole of the Hebrew and Christian Scriptures seems directly concerned with *redemptive* creation—and not originative creation. This redemptive activity involves a whole mega-process of bringing to potential recovery—eventually in the Messiah—self-depressed created persons. The hopeful prospect emerges that, despite their precariously processive existence, these persons will become *willing* to be *awakened* and *receive* restoration. Restoration cannot be done merely *to* them (impersonally). It will have to be fully *received by* them (interpersonally).

The Big Implication

Some people take the *Genesis* story of creation literally; others, symbolically. However it is interpreted, the revelation seems open to the idea that we deserved to inherit the resultant original sin.

If we had not sinned originatively, how could we be in the present predicament? An infinitely good, infinitely powerful, and infinitely creative God would have given us innocent parents, not guilty ones. Rather, there would be no need for parents at all, much less a line of parentage. Realizing that *God's "integrity" is infinite*, we can also be sure that we deserve our present inheritance.

Suppose we were to take the Eden story rather figuratively—at its "root" level. Then it could mean that Adam and Eve had a deeper choice than eating or not eating the fruit of the tree. It could mean symbolically, yet quite really, that they had the choice whether to receive well, or not so well, the gift of being. According to such an interpretation, Adam and Eve, responding to the gift of being-at-all, apparently had some kind of a problem with saying fully "yes."

In this illustrative way of looking at the story, the prime couple had full personhood before God. But they *freely* desired to be the supreme source of their own life. They stumbled over the prospect of being merely finite.

In other words, they fell into making a root-level *contrast*. They compared themselves with *God*. God, however, is entirely beyond *comparison*. Their depth-response was hardly the unconditionally loving gratitude that the gift of being—gifted from the heart of God directly—should evoke, spontaneously, freely, and intimately.

They did not respond generously to their Creator. Instead, it would seem they turned one eye (figuratively speaking) toward themselves. They *freely* diverted themselves away from God. Therefore, we might say that the infinite "difference" (not distance) between their own being and the being of God, actively bringing them to *be*, could have *occasioned* their unwillingness.

This "infinite difference" in *kind* of being could *not* have *caused* their saying *maybe*. Their reluctance to *be* the being God gave them was undertaken freely. But such a difference would have been their freely chosen *excuse* for their (freely) failing will.

At the moment God willed them to be and to be themselves, they must have faltered. As God gave them their whole and perfect finite being, they received it freely by partially denying who they were being gifted to be. They did not fully affirm their being-with God and thereby enter heaven. Neither did they fully say *no* and create a hellish destiny.

To the very act of God, they answered in a less than perfect way. They did so *by the gifted, perfect power of freedom itself.* They must have said, in effect, both *yes* and *no* to the sheer *gift* of being-at-all.

As a result, they became virtually powerless to be who they were. Yet they had *not fully* rejected God and their own being. So, in the divine goodness and mercy, God was able to revive them. This "re-creation" started to occur right from within their already existing, self-decimated being. And *that* creation—creation *ex aliquo* ("out of something")—is taken up by the accounts in the *Book of Genesis*.

The creation stories in *Genesis* then are versions of the beginning of our *remedial or redemptive* creation. Such activity of God is not the creation of the whole being of each person "out of nothing." It is the making of a new and functional *part* of him or her. This newly developed *part* of a crashed creature comprises the functional, soul-body existence within space and time, that is attained at the moment of conception; it serves as a kind of ontological placenta or service organ of the originatively created person.

This serviceable manner of existence in which we are now living is designed to assist in the awakening of the whole person to his or her comatose, crashed condition of being. We failing persons now exist in the self-inflicted darkness that was caused by our originative decision. We need awareness of origins and of the magnitude of our alienation from God.

As one of the Scriptural accounts indicates, the world of matter was gradually formed, "day by day," until it was made ready for the entry of Adam and Eve *as existents in space and time*. According to the new perspective, however, at that point they had already sinned *originatively*.

Their personal *originative* sins *and ours* had created chaos in our being. The creation stories of *Genesis* start from this condition. The first couple was created *ex aliquo*—out of a chaotic state of being.

Only after their original sin in Eden could they and their offspring eventually, or even possibly, come to understanding *why* they were functionally made in Eden and why they were to be banished.

The grossly impersonal cosmos is an orderly formation of passive matter and motion. This "cosmess" of good and evil is something that *we* caused, *not to be*, but to *ex*-ist. This kind of be-ing stands outside itself, is somewhat alien to itself, and "begs" to "return" to the "freedom of the children of God."

The original choice of Adam and Eve, evoked in the Garden, made it *possible* for the coming of much deeper awareness—an awareness of the *being*-based character of our sin and of God's infinitely loving response that includes our redemption and the *opportunity* for our salvation.

Chapter 7

The Condition for Temptation

Taking the *Genesis* story as it appears, we notice that Adam and Eve are *temptable*. The serpent tempted Eve and, through her, Adam.

But we ought to wonder why they were *able* to be tempted at all.

Before the temptation scene in the Garden, already they must have had reservations about something. If they had said fully *yes* to God at the temptationless moment of pure creation, they would have been confirmed within the presence and grace of God, and would have been joyful forever without any interruption.

The completely active potency of their wills to say *yes* would have been fulfilled. There would have been no grounds for a Garden of Eden, nor for a trial—at least not for them. They would have entered into everlasting union with God and with all other created persons who said fully *yes* in responding to God saying *Be*.

Of course, in the act of being created *out of nothing*, if Adam and Eve had said *no*—with their whole hearts—they would have brought upon themselves the everlasting frustration we call hell. The utter possibility that they could willfully fail *completely* would have been realized. They would have *destructured* their own being, quite like multitudes of angelic creatures did to themselves.

Adam and Eve were temptable only because they had at once said, in effect, *maybe* (both *yes* and *no*) to reality. By their inaugural sin at the moment of creation "out of nothing," they had disrupted their own being. They seemed to require this "testing" as to whether they "really meant" their *maybe*—and to whatever extent. Hence, *Genesis* delineates, from its very beginning, God's re-creative recovery: the redemptive creation.

The Temptable Adam and Eve

The temptation in Eden and the fall seems particularly designed so as to make Adam and Eve profoundly aware that they were *not* fully friends with God even before that point. The "test" in the Garden was their wake-up call. "Wake up and *know* your sinfulness."

By choosing to eat the forbidden fruit, they were saying, if not yet consciously, "Yes, we mean the *no* in our *maybe*!" And that should have stirred them to an awareness of their already-repressed, initial reluctance to be the perfect creatures with the perfect freedom they were gifted to be.

By choosing to eat—choosing to commit to the *experience* of evil as well as of good—they committed what has been called *original* sin. The punishment they received made them shockingly aware of their natural weakness. And this weakness of being could only have been caused by their much deeper *originative* sin.

Eating the fruit of a tree just does not signify sufficiently. But this *behavioral origin* of sin reveals the primal less-than-fully-good state of *their* being and of *ours*.

God knew all about their incapacity to be fully faithful. So, Satan, in serpentinian guise, was allowed to tempt them. This fact suggests that they had already constituted themselves to be in a condition of indecision between *yes* and *no*. Their disobedience in the Garden was sure confirmation of the negative in their rudimental *maybe*.

The Garden Story, then, is the dramatic account of Adam and Eve coming-into-*awareness* of their weakness and of their obvious lack of a confirmed union with God. *An originative sin had been totally repressed.*

They were destined to be shaken out of their self-stifled condition. Their disobedience in Eden served to highlight the partly negative disposition toward being-who-they-were that they already had. They must have been placed in the Garden as the consequence of their *originative* sin.

The choice in Eden did not send them to hell. God banished them to live a precarious life on earth and to die. After their original sin, Adam and Eve would undergo a cosmic existence, continuing to be on trial and tested by decisions and by cultivated habits. They were to determine which side of their *maybe*—*yes* or *no*—they would ultimately choose. *No* would lead them into hell; *yes*, into heaven, thanks to the power of God's redeeming Love.

They had been created absolutely *"out of nothing"*—not out of dust or something else. By that originatively creating act, God must have offered an immediate, absolute, and unconditional friendship. God's gift of their being was a perfect gift—in no way partial or conditional.

So, the whole purpose of Eden appears to be designed by God to *raise the consciousness* of primal parents, Adam and Eve. Their presence in the world of space and time had been fashioned from non-living elements (the dust of the earth). There they are put on trial. In that "trying situation," they could *possibly* come to realize that their friendship with God was real, but immensely deficient.

Their disobedience in the Garden was *inevitable* because—at the moment of their common creation with all other persons, human and angelic—they had set themselves up for disobedience. They had *willed* to be distrustful of the being they were gifted to be.

In the Garden scene, there was no consideration of the possibility that, while Eve would say "yes" to the serpent, Adam would say, "no." Nor conversely. And if they had given responses opposite to each other, what kind of world would that have wrought for us? Would we then have come into this world only half as skewed as we are now?

Even to wonder about such a split only underscores how we are so unaware of the gift of *originative freedom*—angelic and human. We are immensely inclined to deny that we were gifted with a perfect freedom—independent of, and beingfully prior to, the basic events of Eden.

Suppose these two progenitors had resisted the evil one and his wiles on the first occasion of temptation. They would still be living on probation, subject to further attempts at provocation. They would continue to exist under the proviso that they dare not eat of the tree of the knowledge of good and evil, lest they be banished and die.

In fact, if they had never succumbed to temptation in the Garden, would they ever have had the opportunity to come into everlasting bliss with God? Would the trial continue *forever*? And would we ever have been born of them? In addition, if children were born in Eden, would some remain faithful and others fall? Then what?

In effect, God "already knew," right at the episode of temptation, that Adam and Eve and all the rest of us had sinned *originatively*. In the first account of creation according to *Genesis*, God is reported as saying, "*Increase and multiply*, and fill the earth, and subdue it, and rule over the fishes of the sea, and the fowls of the air, and all living creatures that move upon the earth" (*Genesis* 1:28). The infinitely perfect Creator is not dealing here with an untrammeled, perfect creation. The originative likeness of these two persons to God is greatly dimmed and barely apparent in the tasks they are given.

The *originative* sin had already been committed. The redemptive world was being arranged by a divine ordering. The first couple and their ensuing offspring were to participate eventually in the struggle to restructure passive-reactive matter. They were even commanded to "subdue it" for the sake of growing in awareness of God, self, and the whole of creation, cosmic and otherwise.

The condition of Adam and Eve in Eden was both blessedness and trial. Their plight was a blessing because they had said *yes* to some degree when first created. Yet there was no confirmed union with God, because they had also said *no* to some degree. The trial loomed indefinitely. After all, they seemed satisfied in Eden, cultivating the soil with ease and eating its yields as they chose.

However, satisfaction—even "heavenly" satisfaction—does not mean fulfillment. They were far from intimate in their love for God and each other. Yet their *no* in the Garden did not condemn them to hell. They did not die on the spot—*physically*. They were expelled: conditioned by the imminent danger of hell.

Mercifully, God set a flaming sword and Cherubim at the entrance to the Garden. This angelic mission prevented these renegades from gaining access to the fruit of the Tree of Life, lest in eating of it they immortalize their sin. At that time, God cryptically suggested that a Redeemer would come to save them and their offspring from their sins, presumably on condition that their hearts would open up to this divine rescue mission.

The predicament of this temptable pair in Eden, even before their temptation and history-originating sin, might be seen by an example of the temptability of children.

People and Pleasure

Children, when entering a candy shop, come with widely varying dispositions. Some would not think of stealing anything. But others come ready to ransack the place. And, of course, most are temptable under certain circumstances.

On the one hand, those who would not even think of stealing are something like Adam and Eve should have been had they not— "prior" to their meeting with the tempter—engaged in a nascent, if partial, unwillingness to be. Actually, if they had not engaged in that initiatory, *untempted* rejection of *full intimacy* with God, they would not have been temptable at all.

Had they been willing fully to be, they would have been confirmed in the goodness of being. Their *yes* to being would have flowed from an unreserved reception of God's unlimited generosity in creating them. No "candy shopping" would be even thinkable. When total intimacy is present, there is no reason for consumption. Consuming could only be *compensation* for lack of intimacy and lack of caring or of being cared for.

On the other hand, children who enter for the purpose of stealing at the first opportunity are like the serpent and like Adam and Eve had they said an unreserved *no* "prior" to entering the Garden. In fact, they probably would not have had the Garden Opportunity at all. By their own ill will, they would have been banished to misery forever without a "chance." There is no question of "pleasure treats" in hell. Self-condemnation renders even consumerism in vain.

Adam and Eve, as described in *Genesis*, are like children who could be tempted to steal in a candy store—though it is not the first thing on their minds. Our first parents presumably were enjoying the gifts of creation around them with the prospect that it could continue indefinitely. They were in God's friendship to some extent. But, like children who are not fully determined to respect the store owner's wishes—especially with the Big Treat in the center of the store that promises an endless supply of candy—Adam and Eve were not fully determined to do God's will.

Why? Why were they not fully disposed to act harmoniously with God? Whatever the specific *reasons*, one necessary *condition* was revealed: they already had a weakness of will that could be preyed upon by malign forces.

How did *that* weakness arise *before the fall*?

Put to the Test

Was it necessary for the sake of their freedom that they be weak at first, so that they could eventually "prove" themselves worthy of communion with God? Was God in the Garden simply testing the noblest creatures of space and time?

Not really. A tester tests only those realities of which there is some *uncertainty*. God, however, could not possibly create or cause to *be* an imperfect anything—anything calling for testing. Only we, who are imperfect makers, have to test our products. God was infinitely certain that *originatively created persons* did not need testing. They were *perfectly* able to determine their own destiny.

It is easy to project, onto God's act of creating perfect creatures, the notion that, in creating us *free*, God had to create us *imperfect*. People are readily persuaded that if we were to be free we had to be temptable and thereby to struggle with decisions. For the *originative* condition, they assume the conditions of already fallen freedom.

Unfortunately, many philosophers and theologians—even from the time of Irenaeus in the second century—have overlooked supreme and perfect finite *freedom*. They have tried to explain the origin of evil in the world by saying that human beings had to "earn" the kingdom of heaven by being tested. They seem to have thought that humans had to have the experience of struggling through trial and error in order to acquire virtue of their own. For many proponents the process is called "soul-making."

Nevertheless, these believers are unaware of the need to recognize an *originative* sin. Their ideas have some merit in an already sinful world and as long as they grant the truth that salvation can only be freely and sincerely *received*, not really *earned*.

We are *redeemed* whether we accept it or not. But we are *saved* only on condition that we are willing to cooperate with the grace of divine redemption. Not everyone who *says*, "I'm saved, I'm saved," is really saved. No matter how many times they say it. Salvation comes only with sincere, heart-gifting commitment to God's saving activity. We can and do readily deceive ourselves.

These considerations of redemption and salvation presuppose the existence of sin. Yet the question of origins is, first of all, concerned with absolute activity, ours as well as God's. The idea that absolute virtue can come in the exercise of a *single act of perfect freedom* does not seem to be found in the considerations of many. They are hidebound by thinking that everything human is to be judged from the perspective of space and time.

Yet how could it be right for the infinitely perfect Creator to "test" free creatures who are created—including their perfect freedom itself—in the divine image and likeness? Their being—with their freedom to be who they are—is perfect, at least before they *act* with it.

None of God's creatures—as they come "from God's hands," so to speak—could be at all imperfect and hence testable. They are finite, limited; *not* infinite, unlimited. But they are *perfect*, finite beings. To think of them as testable, at that point, is to project onto God our egocentric ways of doing things.

Would there be any testing if these creatures had exercised this perfect freedom perfectly, and if they freely had said *yes* to God? No, only those would become testable who—by their first *act* of perfect freedom—freely acted distortedly in exercising the perfect *power* of freedom with which they were created. *In originative creation, there is no temptation.*

Only those who *untemptedly* said, in effect, *maybe* would need to face a test. Which *side* of *maybe*—*yes* or *no*—would they ultimately choose? *Maybe* is an incomplete decision, an incomplete act of self-determination: an imperfect exercise of *perfect* freedom. (The God-gifted, *perfect power* of freedom exercised by any creature is not imperfect before it is perfect. That *power* is perfect as a dimension of the perfect being of the person created by God).

It is the creature who can make self imperfect by means of an *act* of self-violation. The created one does the *act* that is imperfect. The *power* does not act. The person *acts*—perfectly or imperfectly with a God-gifted perfect freedom-power. What becomes imperfect is not the *power* as such—gifted by God—but the *person* who exercises it badly.)

The Perfect Power of Free Love

The gift of perfect freedom, given by God to every finite person, is *not* the *actual* determination itself. This singular gift is the *ability* to determine, within God's Providence, one's own everlasting destiny.

So, then, in order to appreciate why a given creature might have to be tested, we cannot simply consider the gift of perfect freedom. We must look to the only *part* of the creature for which *God is in no way responsible*: *the very content of the actual exercise* of the creature's perfect *power* to be free.

If the created person's first *act* of that perfect freedom is *done* in a finitely *perfect way*, the creature *thereby* freely unites with God—constituting full union of the *gift*-being with the *Giver*-Being. This created person is confirmed in God's friendship forever.

But, instead, this perfect *power* to love wholeheartedly might be disrespected by the one acting with it. A perfect *power* to love—not a perfect *act* of love—might be exercised (in its first *act*) negatively. Thus the acting creature thereby *causes* his or her imperfection "on the spot." *By* the perfect *power* of freedom, a created person *causes* self to be imperfect. The perfect *power* does not cause it; the *person* does it by an *act* that *deforms* the *power* even as it is being received, though not as it is being gifted. (The *power* in question is not just any kind of power or perfection. It is the *power to be free*. Not the power simply to be a walker or a talker. Freedom is really freedom, not fixation. Freedom is the power to *will* freely.)

The resultant damaged condition is effectively one of tempt*ability*. This ability to be tempted, then, is based on a self-caused *functional* lack of perfect freedom—*not on an essential* lack. To the God-gifted perfect power to be free the failing person "adds" imperfection—an imperfect functionality.

Temptability, as well as testability, imply an already distorted and indecisive freedom. There is a susceptibility to further self-maiming. However, even if a person is already somewhat of a transgressor, the stronger in truth and virtue he or she is or becomes, the less effect temptation will have.

In fact, one who is actually perfect in virtue cannot be *effectively* tempted. In such case, any temptation would amount to an act of the tempter; but it would not be a significant threat to the one tempted. The tempted person might well be abused and tormented by the temptation, but not really able to succumb.

For example, if a person is fully grown, strong, and in good health, the blows of a three-year-old might hurt, but cannot knock him or her down. This person might be said to be hit-able by the child, but not fell-able. God is, *as it were*, like that—in an infinite "way." God is offend-able by us, but not defeat-able.

Christians believe that Jesus was "tempted." Nevertheless, they do not believe that he could sin. He *is* God, and God cannot sin or be *effectively* tempted.

Though Jesus suffered from the assaults of the tempter, he was not effectively temptable. It was simply fitting that he be subjected to many kinds of evil—except sin itself and the ability to sin—endured by those he was redeeming. Out of fathomless, self-sacrificial love, he identified as fully as possible with their condition, including their temptations and most appalling sufferings.

From the Christian perspective, the temptations of Jesus could be viewed simply as futile attempts of Satan. They were real acts of temptation on the part of the tempter. But, on the part of the one tempted, they were agonizing blows of temptation that could not possibly be effective. In trying to destroy the purpose of Jesus, the evil one proudly and vainly insinuated that good results would come if his tempting suggestions were followed. Jesus rebuffed Satan by saying that God is not to be tempted.

All theists, Christian or not, believe in the Creator who creates perfectly each individual person. Unfortunately, many *think* of God as an *arbitrary* creator when they *say* God is an *infinite* Creator. But they can come to realize that Adam and Eve and each one of us were not even temptable effectively by Satan upon being created "out of nothing." We were temptable only "after" *the non-temporal, pre-Eden moment, in which we had been gifted with our perfect personal being by infinite Love.*

In that non-durational moment of creation, wherein the heart of God created *all* persons "out of nothing," Satan's refusal to be who God created him to be would *not* have been influential on *any* of us other persons. At *that* moment, this "eventually-evil" presence in creation was not *effectively* a temptation for us, since each person is created in perfect, undamaged freedom, quite capable of giving a full, first, and final *yes.*

God's infinite goodness empowers each perfectly unique person—angelic and human—in the pure exercise of this created, *supremely personal, first act* of freedom. But this is an act that can be done only by the created person—not at all by God or by anyone else.

At that moment, insofar as we *responded* by saying *maybe I will receive the gift of being,* we rendered ourselves vulnerable to the power of evil. We became eminently temptable. Even the slightest "hesitation" or unwillingness would have been incredibly offensive to *infinite* goodness and infinite beauty of divine Love—and greatly harmful to our being.

Only the saving power of God, by the creation cited in *Genesis* and subsequent redemptive action, could save us and afford us total recovery—*with* our cooperation. There must have been at least some flicker of *yes* abiding in our hearts, with which God could work, to effect our redemptive creation and, if we are willing, our salvation.

Because of God's infinite power and goodness, even the slightest willingness to be saved can be enough to start the process, however long or short it might be. God's infinite mercy can sustain whatever is needed.

The Attitude of Real Temptability

In any event, the temptations of Adam and Eve in the Garden were real. Not only on the part of Satan, but also on their part. If our first parents had resisted temptation coming to them through the serpent, presumably they could have prolonged their stay in the Garden. But the prideful tempter would have continued his efforts to overcome their resistance.

Adam and Eve gave little, if any, opposition to the serpent. They thereby revealed their incapability in the long run.

The *Genesis* story reveals a disposition toward a "me-first" choice. Like the kind of children temptable under certain conditions in a candy store, Adam and Eve, without wavering, and under a certain pretext, stole from the "owner." They proved themselves not only unwelcome in the Garden, but also, at that juncture, incapable of genuine friendship with God. And so they were driven out.

Their act of monumental "shoplifting" manifests how they were disposed to it by an *attitude* with which they must have entered: "God put me here, I surely did not. None of this is mine. God owns everything. Why cannot I own something, too? Why merely share what is God's, as God wants me to do? Why not have something that is mine as well, such as this opportunity to know (experience) good and evil for myself?"

And so Adam and Eve got what they wanted. However, they also got what they had not anticipated: consequences that cut to the core of their being and freedom. As happiness or fulfillment results from doing what is good, sadness follows from doing what is bad. Indeed, evildoing causes sadness and the conditions for ongoing frustration.

Multiplicities of pain and suffering are the results of evil. These miseries are the voices of meaninglessness. Suffering can become redemptive and meaningful, but only after repentance that includes a willingness to change our hearts—in, through, and by *that suffering.*

A responsible proprietor of a lavish candy store does not want to test or tempt any shopper. Attractive displays are set up to garner business that respects product and property. The owner might desire floorwalkers and clerks having wary eyes. But good clerks serve mainly by facilitating transactions, not temptations.

The Supreme Gardener, however, allowed an evil spirit on the premises in order to test the first resident-consumers, bringing to their awareness their lack of integrity. Issues were to be resolved. Could the residents be faithful in "little things," like not stealing, that they might be set over greater things? Or would they fail the test and deserve the resulting self-inflicted pain?

When put to the test, Adam and Eve failed on the spot. They were an easy prey for the wily, ravenous forces of evil. The impulsiveness of their decision portrayed by *Genesis* strongly suggests that their story, as we have known it, leaves something momentous *untold*. Their "original choice" in Eden had deep roots in their very *being*. We would do well to expose further these roots, hidden below the surface of *Genesis*.

Chapter 8

There is More to This Story

People like to get "the inside story" on the news.

When hearing some media report, we wonder how the event really happened. Not only *what* happened—not merely the basic facts of the case. We like to know how and why the main players acted as they did. The "inside story" helps us to identify with some of the central characters and the meaning of their actions. And there can be several versions.

The real "inside" story, however, is often difficult to get. Personal and social interests of the various parties involved readily obstruct objective attempts to break into the heart of a news story.

Perhaps the Good News of redemption and potential salvation is not entirely exceptional in this respect. The "Full Story" might be hidden by the self-interests of many of the parties involved, namely, all of us. Standard interpretations of the story of origins in the *Book of Genesis* seem to give, for the most part, an "outside story." We seem to be on the outside looking in. Such a view itself is good, but requires ever-deeper penetration.

We also need to try to get the "inside story" on the Good News. Such would not purport to be a "privileged knowledge," as in the futile attempts of Gnosticism throughout history. The knowledge could be gained by any sincere believer using reason in the exercise of faith. At least, we can make a serious attempt by using common sense and then by developing, *from within common sense*, a refined or *uncommon* sense.

For instance, we notice that Eve did not try to resist Satan. She seemed disloyal to God without a second thought. The first woman was quite susceptible to deception. She was imperfect even before the temptation began.

Yet God's infinite power and goodness created her whole—able to know and love finitely, yet perfectly, and to be fully free. Therefore, *she* must have done something to weaken her intellect and will, and her whole being, "before" her encounter with *any* tempter. (Here the word "before" does not *signify* a priority with respect to time. Her *first* response to creation could not have been a temporal act. Time itself is one *result* of giving immediately the *maybe* response. That *maybe-saying* causes time, and much else.)

By virtue of the act of God, Eve did not come with a weakness of willpower. Her functional infirmity of will had to have been self-inflicted—through her distortion of gifted primal *freedom*. She must have had, at first, within her being as God immediately gifted it, *no* weakness of will*power*. Nevertheless, *by way of* her first *act with* that perfect natural *power* to say *yes* fully, *she* fell freely short.

Our wills do not sin. *We* do. We do so by *doing* our willing badly.

Apparently, Adam actually offered little or no resistance to Eve. He seemed to be disloyal to God without asking a single question. Adam was the original wimp. If he was created perfect, as many believe, then somewhere "between" his originative creation by God and the temptation scene he must have damaged his power to see and to be completely self-directive. The only point for such damage to occur was in his original act of *personally receiving* his *being* at the moment of creation.

Genesis does not *report* how Adam and Eve had character flaws that made them quite vulnerable to the tempter. Nonetheless, the text and context seem to portray their moral fiber as defective, whereby they were disinclined to resist. Granted that they succumbed to the temptation, why did they not, at least, put up a fight? In any case, we do not get a sense of their nature as perfectly free.

A *perfectly* free person is created with the complete freedom to love wholeheartedly God and all others and is one who *actually does fully exercise* that freedom *immediately*. If Adam and Eve were perfectly free in the Garden, having fully willed who they were, in accord with God's gift of being, they would not have been able to be deceived by anyone. They would have readily and confidently held to God's command. Indeed, tempting or testing them would have been in vain. (They would have had no "business" in the Garden.)

Adam and Eve, however, had a weakness in their disposition—a *defectiveness* of both understanding and willing. If God were to have created them with this debility, God would be a defective Creator. But if God did not create Adam and Eve with a character flaw, how did the deficiency get there before the serpent arrived? Whether we assume that the story is to be taken as quite literal in significance or that it is to be regarded as largely symbolic, there must be more to the actions of Adam and Eve than is usually recognized.

In the Garden, Where Is the Love?

Right from the start, Adam and Eve seem to have been lacking in their commitment to God and in their *capacity* to detect deception. They seem to be acting like love-deprived children, substituting the consumption of goodies (forbidden fruit) for the real good they most deeply need.

Children often have difficult times in our present imperfect world. Sometimes they are warned not to do what is harmful, yet they do it anyway. The problem can be a lack of feeling loved by their parents.

When they disobey in spite of "having everything," they might not be satisfied by the largely material abundance they already have. Their susceptibility to temptation might indicate the need for more affection and security—for genuinely affirming love.

Here on earth, the children themselves may be to blame as much as the parents. After all, like their parents, they come into the world driven by innate selfishness and enwrapped with varying measures of insensitivity to what is genuine love. Their parents, of course, have immense responsibility for education and discipline conducted in a climate of unconditional love. And they often fail. Yet children and parents can end up rightly sharing the blame for family failures.

But God is *never* to blame for any lack of affirming love. So, in our first parents, the absence of a fully loving attitude toward God could only have come about through their own unwillingness to receive fully the gifted divine love and the intimacy. This love was immediately present to them from the moment of creation "out of nothing." When God declared, "Be," they were *infinitely and freely* affirmed.

In the Garden of Eden, however, Adam and Eve acted somewhat like adolescents. Many teen-agers are not always content with dates, parties, and shared good times with friends. Out of some misdirected hunger for genuine love, they reach for sex. Similarly, Adam and Eve appeared too ready to substitute something else for love.

The first man and woman do not show themselves to be fulfilled by all they have in the lifestyle of Eden. Perhaps they were not even satisfied with each other. They might have been reaching for the forbidden fruit out of craving much greater closeness to each other and to God. Eve had been the remedy for Adam's loneliness. She fulfilled his needs for a companion, but not perhaps his needs for love and friendship. Nor was he sufficient for *her* needs.

Where was intimate love in the Garden scene? Where was the love and sincere concern for God and for each other? Apparently, with hardly any deliberation, both Eve and Adam grabbed at the chance to satisfy immediate desires instead of living peacefully within their relationship with God.

The evil one easily persuaded them that God was *not* on their side. He induced them to think that God was trying to prevent them from being "God-like" in knowing good and evil. But how could they so quickly believe a lie about one whom they loved? And from whom they felt infinite love? Most importantly, where was *their* love?

Good or bad behavior branches forth from good or bad character. Both behavior and character, however, are rooted in *being*. Freedom to *do* what is good comes from freedom to *be* what we ought to *be*. The breakable character of the pair in the Garden reveals weakness in their *being*, the cause of their eventual shame.

If Adam and Eve had actually refused to eat the prohibited fruit, they would have strengthened their character and their ability to resist evil. They would have given their roots new depth within the ground of being, at least for a while. However, they had apparently "already" made a decision *about* their *roots* and *from* their roots.

They seem to have a take-it-for-granted attitude toward who and what they are, and toward their being-at-all. They seem too much like us in our matter-of-factness about the gift of being "out of nothing." The Adam and Eve of *Genesis* seem like children who do not know who they are or why they exist, and who want to get the best for themselves. Just like the rest of us.

Where then do we find the love in Eden? There were pleasures and principles, satisfactions and commandments. Nevertheless, *intimacy* was lacking between man and woman, and between them and God.

Genesis does not show that Adam and Eve had formed an intimate communion of friends. It shows persons conversant with each other. They are companions in exploration, but not necessarily committed. The inhabitants of Eden seem strangely disposed for alienation.

We might ask whether the ancient writers of *Genesis* and of other Biblical works had, themselves, a capacity for intimacy. Could they convey the spontaneous closeness of loving relationships through Biblical characters like Adam and Eve in the Garden?

Obviously, every human writer has a weakened sense of intimacy and love, just as we readers do. The human, instrumental author of *Genesis* was, after all, a child of Adam and Eve, distant from the infamous surrender to the serpent. Yet the Scriptures are the word of God, who is infinite Love. In the texts, through struggling human agents, "God writes straight with crooked lines."

The original sin committed in the Garden affects us all, even as we are now reading or writing about the origin of creation, evil, and redemption. So we can only wonder what the potential of Adam and Eve really was. At any rate, we are called to deepen our insight to the best of our ability: through prayerful contemplation.

We can realize today how the Garden Story, as it is told, lacks a sense of intimacy between Adam, Eve, and God. At least, from the *historical* perspective, such deficiency did not *originate* with certain subsequent children of Adam and Eve. The teller of the story was not the origin.

The deficiency was in the protagonists themselves. The moral and spiritual character that they were missing became especially evident when they directly disobeyed the will of God by so thoughtlessly and heartlessly eating the forbidden fruit.

Where Is the *Creator*?

In the story, Adam and Eve are somewhat lacking in love for God. But it would also *seem* that God's love for all creation was missing from the start.

God is not portrayed as the perfect Creator, creating each person singly and all persons communally with an infinitely intimate and interpersonal love. God is not depicted as the truly perfect Creator, bringing to be—"out of nothing"—the fullness and perfect being of every person. God's human creatures are not taken to be *able* to love *immediately* and *completely* their Creator God by a rapturous union forever.

Creation *out of nothing* is a free, loving call into total being-at-all. Nonetheless, *Genesis* begins with God fashioning the heavens and the earth, and then all living creatures. The activity is more an effort of *making* than of creating.

Making is producing something out of something. Creating is an effortless gifting of being "out of nothing." Making is essentially a process. But c*reating* is *not* a process at all, but the *free, absolute, unconditional act of loving someone fully and perfectly into being.*

Creating is *gifting*. There is nothing passive in this infinite *gifting* activity. It is *not* donating, delivering, producing, or the like that would require the involvement of passivity.

When fallen humans make something, they work on materials and form them into particular structures. They take conditions and re-condition them.

A baker takes flour, water, yeast, and salt, and then rolls them together, applying the heat of a stove to produce bread. A sculptor takes wood and knife and cuts away at the wood to produce a statue. A poet takes paper, ink, and words, and shapes them into a poem. We can say that the baker, sculptor, and poet *create* because of the way they bring out *new* structures and forms. Nevertheless, they do not strictly create; they make. The "new" forms are brought out of stuff having "old" forms.

Creation, in contrast, is a *bringing to be* something wholly fresh, without any pre-existing materials or forms *whatsoever*. The result of creation is something *entirely* new. *All* of the being of a created person comes "out of nothing" by the act of God alone.

Yet no *created* person can create "out of nothing," because the creature, *by virtue of himself or herself*, really is not. (By virtue of being God's gift, however, each created person—whether angelic or human—is an unique magnificence, awesome to contemplate.) The creature, *as creature*, simply has no *being by necessity*, and hence cannot give new or "additional" *being* to any other. New *becoming*, yes; new *being*, no.

Parents do not create or even cause the *being* of their children. As decisive actors in the *coming-to-exist* of their children, they act "pro-creatively." They are causes of becoming, not of being. They cannot give *being* to the child because they have had no say as to whether they themselves would be at all or not. Like their children, they *are* because God says so and not at all because they say so.

The descriptions of creation in *Genesis* highlight God's necessary involvement in the *coming* to be of the heavens and the earth, the plants and animals, the Garden of Eden, and the man and woman. In *Jeremiah* (18:1-8), Yahweh God is even compared to a potter who is reworking bad pots. Nevertheless, no attempt is undertaken to refer directly to what later theistic reflection recognizes as the heart of God's creative act: the absolute *gifting* of being-at-all, and of being this unique one and not any other.

Even today, many philosophers and theologians fail to recognize the crucial difference between being and becoming. They regularly treat evolution, for instance, as though it were creation. Instead, they ought to recognize that, even if they think there might be some truth in cosmic processes being evolutional, evolution itself would be essentially a be-*coming*. This coming-to-*exist* would not be simply a coming-to-*be*. Evolution would represent a clear *manifestation* of a certain *kind* of being—of an *existence in recovery*.

How something *comes* to exist or "becomes itself" is not the same as whether it *is* at all. Coming to exist, or becoming, is a process or part of a process. But be-*ing* or being-at-all is radically different.

God making Adam out of the dust and Eve out of a rib to live in the Garden is not the same as God creating Adam and Eve "out of nothing"—gifting them fully to *be* "from the Heart." Creation from nothing means that there is nothing "between" the Creator and the creature. *No thing* (nothing) mediates their relationship. They relate, *immediately and fully.*

Making, however, means that there *is* indeed something between the cause and the effect. In the process of making, some other beings or elements are used to bring about the new "being."

However, in the originative creation of *being*—before the process of becoming could ever occur—there is *nothing between* God, the cause, and us, the effects. By our own originative, sinful response, however, we have placed plenty "between" God and ourselves.

Typically, we have it wrong in our consciousness. We think things have to become in order to be. However, the reverse is much truer: things really have to *be* before they can *become*—if any becoming (process) is *needed*.

Becoming is solely based in being; not being in becoming. Every becoming is itself a *being*, but not every being is a *becoming*. God is not a becoming, nor are the proper effects of God. Today's "process theologians" are looking through the wrong end of what might be called intellectiscopes: ontological "telescopes" or "microscopes."

The descriptions in *Genesis* suggest more about a Maker than they do about a Creator. This Maker of the heavens and the earth uses existing things to make new things. Out of the void that was earth and out of the darkness of the deep, God brought forth light. There was a vault made that divided the waters, and much more. Adam was brought forth from the dust and Eve from the rib of Adam. That is what the *Maker* did. So, where is the *Creator*?

Where Is the Absolutely *Original* Creation?

There are hints of an original creation story behind the events in *Genesis*. Eve confronted the presence of a talking, scheming spirit in the guise of a serpent. After the fall, Cherubim took a stance in front of Eden (*Genesis* 3:24). These spiritual creatures are superior to the human. They must have been created differently from the human couple in the Garden. Reading further, we notice more references to angels appearing in various pages of Scripture.

We might ask, then, "How and when were the angels created?" Why do they not appear within the first lines of *Genesis*? Obviously, their part of the creation story is left untold. Perhaps the account of their auspicious beginning does not serve directly our egocentric, anthropocentric, and redemptive interests.

Augustine and other theologians have tried to associate, with the creation of the angels, the appearance of "light" near the beginning of the *Genesis* story. Nevertheless, even if the word, "heavens," in the first sentence of the Bible somehow refers to the creation of the angels, and not simply to the cosmic skies, where is the specific significance?

Theologians rightly speculate. The angels are vividly presented in a number of Biblical texts either as practical spiritual helpers on behalf of human redemption or as serious threats of damnation—as in the case of Eden's serpent. Nevertheless, the *origins* of all angels and of the life of the good angels with God are given scant attention. (The anagogical readings of texts by Augustine and others constitute an important enrichment of Biblical perspective, but cannot make up for our deficiency in ontological knowledge.)

Scriptural writers do not attend to what had to be the *absolutely interpersonal* creation of each person—whether angelic or human. Likewise, they are disinclined to speak of the inner life of angelic persons. For their purposes of proclaiming the good news, creation by God as the Maker-Redeemer, supersedes all other considerations. They do not ever represent directly what must have been the unitary creation of *all* persons—angelic and human *together*.

Searching, then, underneath *Genesis*, into the roots of the story, we can reach toward the Creator behind the Maker. We also need to cherish the love behind the "Don't you dare!" in the Garden. The loving Creator, beyond all effort and making, creates finite persons to love and to receive in love. God's infinitely personal love creates them *all* immediately "out of nothing."

God is supremely personal—*nothing but* Personhood. God is in no way some*thing*. So, we can come to realize that this originative creation was essentially, immediately, and totally an *inter*personal activity or "event." Only persons were involved, *and all at once—*

no temporal or spatial dimensions whatsoever. Finite persons were brought into being in the likeness of the infinite Person (Hebrew and Islamic belief) or the triune infinite Persons (Christian belief).

In this supreme, perfect creation—"fresh from the heart of God"—there were no inherently imperfect creatures, such as rocks, water, plants, and animals. And certainly there was no void. All created beings were *perfect kinds* of being. None were kinds of being that were inherently defective, though spectacular according to our fallen standards. All creatures in this first creation, therefore, were *persons and only persons*—angelic and human.

Where is the story of this *primal* creation? Where is the perfect creation, immediately and fully resulting in completely free persons? Such beings *could* respond freely, directly, immediately, and fully to the Person(s) of God in supreme intimacy: being-with-Being.

Were *we* included in this *originative* creation? We can think that we were *not*; but that is only if we project onto God and God's most intimate Ways our inherently imperfect ways in space and time.

Theistic people realize that God is not a demiurge, working only with some kind of matter to give it new forms. God is Person-all, in Being and in Activity.

So, we can conclude our present wondering about the story of creation by raising a crucial question.

Suppose that humans were *not* included in the originative creation of perfect persons. Suppose they were created simply as portrayed in *Genesis*. There they are said to come to be only after the creation of many forms of imperfect entities—in six days, whether literally or figuratively. Then we would be faced with a huge fracture within the community of created *persons*.

Angels and humans would have been created within quite separate endeavors of God. But does God "space out" into parts the beings that are given to be by the activity of the divine Interior? Is God like a human creator?

How can we come to see angels and humans as more intimately related at their origins? Between these two kinds of created persons, there is such a bewildering chasm. Where could the *break in being* come from? From God?

Our basic response would have to be: no, only from us. God could not have allowed *perfectly innocent* beings to suffer the slightest evil against their good will. Much less would they be allowed to suffer unjustly through the deluge of physical, psychological, and moral evil involved in the world of space and time.

So, *we* must be far from perfectly innocent persons. The cataclysm must be self-inflicted, coming from the self-negating exercise of our perfect personal power to determine what kind of human persons we *will* to be.

That self-diminishing, yet somewhat self-affirming, first act of our freedom—responding to God, person-to-Person—involved at least a partial unwillingness to be as God was gifting us to be. It should not be surprising *now* that this first *inter*personal act of ours is massively repressed. How could one suppose that, if it occurred, it would *not* be repressed? How could we *dare to let ourselves know it*?

Our present condition of *being* is one of substantial repression. As a result, we read the story of *Genesis* such that we think it to be the story of *originative* creation. We have not recognized how fully it is the story of *redemptive* creation. It does not reveal—except by the questions it occasions—an originative creation. Rather, it describes a reparative, reformative, restorative creation.

We need to discern how the *Book of Genesis*—and the whole of Biblical revelation—tells not so much about our *being*, but about the *coming* of our being here, in the world of our be-*coming*. The Bible reveals the whole process of our recovery and of our coming to be *ontologically rehabilitated* by God's infinitely redeeming Love.

Right within the *Genesis* story, as well as around it, are found intimations of more than is told explicitly. This story of the trunk of the tree of "free choice" can lead us to explore the roots. These roots lead us into the *heart* of God, the only *Giver* of our being-at-all.

Other points of the Christian Scripture touch on our origin in God as apparently much more intimate. In *Ephesians* 1:4, we read how God knew and chose each one of us before the foundation of the world and that we were called to be holy and blameless in the divine love. In other words, we come by the activity of God's heart before we come by any activity in a Garden.

Nonetheless, the *Book of Genesis* teems with significance. Readers must go beyond the *linear* meanings, whether literal or figurative. We need, in our hearts, to relate with our own personal involvement in the origins. That is where the "inside story" really begins.

Chapter 9

The Origins of Humility

Creation *out of nothing* is an interpersonal act of God. The Person of God, or the (Triune) Persons, infinitely intended our being-at-all and our immediate, free response. We were absolutely gifted to be and to *be-with* the Eternal Person(s) forever. If we can bring ourselves to realize the incomparable gift of being and of being perfect persons within the divine Communion, we will be joyful and humble, ever more than we have become so far.

Our redemption will pierce us to the heart of our sorrow, as well as our joy. We know that we know more than we consciously know. We know, at least unconsciously, that we are profoundly responsible *personally* for our very *being-in* a subjunctive, supplementary world caused by originative evil.

We still might not be ready to believe it consciously. But if we do not believe that we sinned originatively with Adam and Eve, we will necessarily—*unconsciously*, and perhaps also consciously—hold something against God who "*put* us" here. Our primal grudge will amount to a stance of *unconsciously* regarding God as "an abusive Parent." Hardly an attitude of humility.

We may never really start to blame God consciously. As a result, the basically unconscious, repressed blaming is bound to continue unabated. The depths of our pride and the unacknowledged pits of selfishness will impede our way to holiness and wholeness of life.

Explanations That Satisfy

In ordinary life, we are inclined to be satisfied with homey ideas of how we got here and how God will save us. Sometimes these familiar thoughts can seem adequate.

A legend illustrates our good-willed, but misguided attempts to portray our situation. I have put it into verse:

The story is told of a Chieftain quite old
Who was wise in the ways of all virtue.
Once he was asked, "Why should you believe
And praise God when life greatly hurts you?"

The Chief thought he could teach and his hearers could reach
The meaning of what we're to hope in.
So, he took some dry twigs, which he piled in a circle,
Taking care that the middle be open.

Then into the center an insect did enter,
Thrust there by the wise old Chief.
Next he started a fire, burning the twigs,
That put the caterpillar to grief.

For the fire burnt fast—an infernal blast
At this insect surrounded by flame.
As the fire progressed the creature obsessed,
Neither exit nor space could it claim.

In one final reaching as though 'twas beseeching,
The woolly insect stretched off the ground
With its head arched upward and trembling feebly
All at once a long finger it found.

Like climbing a tree, this creature went free

With the critical help of a schemer.

Yes, the finger belonged to the tribal sage,

Who was teaching how God's our Redeemer.

"Praise God," the Chief said, "That when we were dead

God looked with compassion and yearning.

Then he sent his Son to teach us his love

And to reach down to save us from burning."

Beautiful image. But we are not at all insects. We are not even *like* insects, except in a superficial way. If anything, insects are like *us* in our *physicalistic* life.

There is no real spirituality to a caterpillar even when it becomes a butterfly. But there might be a dull likeness to human recuperative spirituality.

So, God *could* not relate to us the way the Chief treated the insect. We are persons created by infinite Love "out of nothing." The way God saves us has *no* real likeness to the way that we might save an insect, under any conditions.

Of course, the way we might save any other *person* in an authentic manner—say, by rescue from drowning after a boating accident—is undoubtedly a bit *like* the way God saves us, except that God's way is infinitely more efficacious.

Even our most courageous, heroic person-to-person efforts hardly compare with God's. Yet, we try to do the best we can to see a likeness. Unfortunately, because of our wounded human nature, we often do not succeed in making reasonably effective adjustments to our perspectives.

The idea of God as like one of us human persons is filled with difficulty. We are called to be faithful to the personhood of God, but we ought not to think of the divinity as being merely our finite kind of personhood immeasurably magnified. We have to attempt to be faithful to our deepest intuitions about how we are somewhat like God's personhood, in our own finite and defective ways.

Suppose that a person whom you love permitted, or even planned for, someone to set your house on fire. Then that first person, who allowed this, saved you, according to plan, at the last minute from the flaming building.

You would feel extremely grateful. But, secretly at least, upon becoming aware of the scheme, you would necessarily resent that "beloved" person's carelessness in allowing this whole ordeal to happen to you in the first place.

Resentment would hinder your growth in respect to your "savior." Your friendship would become cooler, at least.

Similarly, with respect to unending salvation, our friendship with God is hampered by our shortsighted view. The *basic interpretation* of creation and of the sin in Eden fails to account *adequately* either for the infinite freedom and power of God or for our own perfect freedom and power as God's beloved creatures. It requires us to infer that God permitted us "innocents" to be thrust into the circle of the parenthood of Adam and Eve, the first sinners.

The theistic revelation of the God of Abraham, of Jesus, and of Mohammed has been taken to imply that God *had* to create us subject to Adam and Eve as our first parents. But, by this way of thinking, we keep ourselves locked into a reticent receptivity in the face of divine Revelation.

We are not receiving fully what it means for God to covenant with personal creation. We are misleading ourselves into thinking that the fault of Adam and Eve was something God planned or permitted us to suffer, but then exercised a divine rescuing and saving power on our behalf.

Oh, Happy Fault

Many Christians, for instance, even have in their liturgy the idea of Adam's sin being a "happy fault that brought so great a Savior."

The expression is considerably true. What could be "greater" than being saved by an infinitely loving Person? But it would also seem to require that we confine ourselves to thinking that our absolute beginning *to be* is the *same* as our functional beginning in the world of space and time.

We are really thought to be ourselves, from the beginning, *only* as children of Adam and Eve. But such an assumption simply does not include a needful perspective on the absolute gift of being *ex nihilo*. Through that absolutely original creation we were gifted to be as *perfect* as we could possibly *be*, and *without any need of parents*.

It might be that most Christians take the "happy fault" designation rather literally, instead of celebrationally. They do not see Adam's sin as transpiring within the context of a mega-calamitous, original disobedience on the part of *all* concerned.

The "happy fault" attitude, if taken literally, would seem to be an excessively "positive" way of evaluating our sin—a way opposite to that of treating the original sin as a "curse" causing us to wallow in woe. Both attitudes—original sin as a "blessing" and as a "curse"— are self-centered and self-affected. Pride preens itself in subtle ways.

Our Relation to "Nothingness" and Our Likeness to God

Humility is rooted in truth, and not simply in self-abnegation. We ought to be humble *primarily* by realizing that we are created "out of nothing" by an infinitely loving Person (or Persons). This infinite Being immediately gives us perfect finite freedom and power for total intimacy.

We are now unconsciously and preconsciously awed by the *being* of that infinite love and also by our inability or unwillingness freely to let it be present to us and to relate with it.

We are not, however, inclined toward the depths of humility. Each of us is more apt, in suffering, to cry out with the spirit of Job, "What have I done to You, O Lord, my God?"

Christians who pray before an image of the crucified Savior are just as apt to wonder, "How could *I* have done *this* to you, Lord?" Or, at least, "How could any infant who dies prematurely have done this to you, Lord?" The largely unconscious inference can readily be, "As a child, I must have been innocent of *this*."

Then the self-hidden questions are likely to include: "How can you do this to me, Lord? How can you be so cruel as to make me suffer when I am innocent—at least innocent of the *origin* of evil in this world?"

Instead of protesting with a "why me" attitude, a humbler heart would say, "Lord, I am not an innocent one; only you are innocent. I do not fully know *how* I am responsible for the cruelty you suffered, but it *must* be so. The torture did not happen by chance.

"I now receive your ever-redeeming love and forgiveness into the depths of myself where I am still in need of functional receptivity. With your infinitely redeeming love, I can receive well both the good and the bad—even the horrendous evils—that might come to me."

We could not really create ourselves "out of nothing" as the magnificently perfect persons with total freedom that we were given to be. Therefore, humility begins with the truth that, *by virtue of ourselves*, we *are not*. It continues with the growing awareness that by poorly receiving the gift of being—by rejecting *full* covenant in creation—we made ourselves profoundly "close to nothing."

We are who we are simply as created persons—as sheer gifts of God to ourselves. We are now awakening to the reality of having *made ourselves* inadequate gifts.

Being who we are is humbling. We subconsciously want to *be* God, instead of simply being *like* God. And we can find ourselves compensating for not being-God by engaging in self-actualization, self-fulfillment, self-esteem, self-affirmation, and other popularly-recommended endeavors. These engagements amount to trying to be like *ourselves*, rather than like *God*. We find ourselves trying to be what *we want* to be, rather than what *God wills* us to be.

We are the ones with the primal wound. We are skewed by the *originative* sin. So, if we *concentrate* on being like ourselves or on "being ourselves," we are founding our endeavors on a false "self."

The crucial endeavor of receiving well our *be*-ing—trying to *be* our be-ing and yet *be* like God—challenges the structure of created being.

The willingness is only mine. Will I be who I am gifted to be, and thereby *be like God*? Or will I be satisfied to be the skewed image of myself that I inevitably chase? My ultimate response is absolutely momentous. Either way of answering determines my final destiny.

Dimming Our Prayer

Our very presence in this world makes it difficult to become aware of our originative response to being. Our preconscious (spiritually unconscious) life is so immense, and our conscious life so small by comparison. We are steeped in a deep mist of *being*—an ontological fog. We are oblivious to our having made, at creation, the super-conscious determination to be somewhat *other than* the being that we *are*.

We can even show our blindness in prayer, such as when we cry out, "Lord, have mercy!"

At times, this common expression can sound as though we are appealing to a human judge who does not fully realize the enormity of our *need* for mercy. God is addressed as a kind of grandiose, yet limited, donor of mercy, who is being called to dispense mercy this way and that way, to this one and that one.

We do not seem to know whom we are addressing. But we must somehow increase our awareness that infinite Mercy acting *infinitely* "has distributed" and "is distributing," *at every moment*, more than sufficient mercy *to everyone*, even the most apparently abandoned. Unlimited mercy is ours for the request and for an active reception of it.

What we intend to say, perhaps, is something humbler and more fitting: "Lord, I *receive,* more and more deeply and gratefully, your unbounded mercy. I receive your infinite mercy within myself and on behalf of others" (who might not be attending to divine mercy or appreciating it).

The air we breathe is teeming with God's mercy and this should be acknowledged in the depths of our hardened souls. We need mercy, but we fail to realize that the mercy is entirely here and now. And an effective *yes* to receiving this ever-accessible, infinite mercy comes only with difficulty, because it must come from the heart of our self-benumbed being.

If the prayer is taken rather literally, "Lord, have mercy" portrays our being entrenched within passive potency and reveals our lack of commitment to God's gift of purely *active* potency, the ability to *do* something. The question is not one of God giving anything more, but of our *receiving*. It would be much better were we to think and even say, "Lord, thank you. *We receive* your infinite, eternal mercy and love."

Otherwise, we are too likely to be bound into meaning something like, "Hey, Lord, hit us with some of your mercy," thinking that mercy is something that God has to *do to* us. We treat ourselves simply as passive potencies at heart, asking to be "done to" by God, instead of increasing the intensity of our acts of *be*-ing, *lov*-ing, *do*-ing, *receiv*-ing.

God is doing God's "infinite best." We are the only ones lagging on the mercy front. But we flee from having to expose ourselves to the truth that our *condition* of passive potency and of *unreceived* mercy comes *ultimately only from ourselves*.

Similarly, when I say, "God bless you" or "God be with you," I really mean virtually the opposite. God *is* infinitely blessing you and is *with* you continuously. *That* is sure. The only wish is that *you* "*Receive* God's blessing" and "*Be* with God."

The typical aspiration, "May God bless you," is founded almost literally on our *maybe-saying* ways. But we can do better. Pivoting from our growing *yes*, we might rather say something like, "May you *receive* God's infinite, *ever-present* blessing!"

Or, at least, we could say, "I bless you, in the name of the Lord," or some such phrasing, where it is clear that any doubt about the efficacy is based on the created person who is doing or receiving the blessing. *God is always blessing everyone infinitely.*

We are stymied because we do not know how to *be* the disabled persons we are by virtue of ourselves *and also* how we can *be* the radiance of being that we *are* in the likeness of God. It would seem, then, that contemplating in prayer the humility of God, our Savior, is the only way to realize the paradoxical truth.

In God's *infinite* majesty of love and compassion, we can keep living the truth of our graced lowliness. We who are "creatures of the maybe" can directly confront our deepest resentments about being susceptible to shocks of a lifetime. By the light of profound sorrow we can let our indignation gradually melt into an everlasting, unconditionally receptive *yes* in likeness to God.

Justice, Fairness, and Mercy

The melting of egocentrism in this world will come only through suffering. We would-be voluntary sufferers, however, are so self-centered that most of the affliction, anguish, and heartache can seem to be totally "unfair."

But fairness is one thing. Justice is quite another.

The Christian parable of the workers in the vineyard suggests a meaning for justice that we might indeed regard as unfair. Jesus said that all the workers were paid the same agreed-upon wage at the end of the day, though some had borne the day's heat and others had worked only the last hour. Because each one agreed upon the wage before entering employment, it was just.

But since some worked many hours and others only one hour, we see it as unjust. We forget that God's justice goes to the core of each person's *freedom*. Together with divine mercy, this justice seems infinitely beyond our comprehension. So, we might discover the "details" of both justice and mercy only in the life to come.

Christians and others, for instance, believe that, even for the most hardened criminals, deathbed conversions are possible. Therefore, those who were faithful to the Gospel over a long life can hardly complain about the apparent ease with which latecomers can attain heaven. Believers know that real justice transcends fairness. God's justice cannot be judged simply by rules of impartiality.

We can begin to acknowledge the difference between justice and fairness when we see that, between thieves, there can be fairness, but not justice. Two persons who agree to rob a bank might split the loot fairly, according to their prior agreements. There is a kind of "honor among thieves." But the whole enterprise—with their very possession of the money, not to mention their distribution of it—is unjust.

Similarly, we are called to see something momentous. We are here on earth, suffering-unto-death justly, while complaining constantly of being treated unfairly.

Once I recognize how personal and radical is my responsibility for my condition of *being in* this world of good-and-evil, my meanings for justice and fairness change. I can then accept all my pains and problems as totally just, no matter how unfair they might seem at the time. Even if I would have to suffer more than anyone else, my complaints about "too much," though emotionally understandable, would be ultimately un*just*ifiable.

I would still not be accepting fully what I first created out of my own being. For saying, even if slightly, *maybe* to the gift of being, I have become self-directed toward a possible separation from divine Life forever.

By virtue of the *no* within the *maybe*, there is nothing in that self-wrought condition itself that could hold me from slipping gradually, or even plummeting, within an abyss of worse-than-nothingness. I could be heading into a creational "black hole" from which escape, on my own or by help from mere creatures—even the totality of created persons—would be impossible.

But as it is, God's mercy still protects me.

Even Job somehow knew this merciful justice, though he suffered "unjustly" or "unfairly" in this world. He was brought to realize how God knew infinitely more than he about why he had to experience decimating losses.

Furthermore, there is nothing that says God's *justice* is limited to life in this world. Those who do not carry, in this life, the full weight of their own good and evil attitudes might experience pain after death. Purgation in a post-mortal world might well be awaiting even those who are now living reasonably "good" lives.

Faith in God opens us to justification. But God alone justifies us. Only God can save us from our original darkening choice. Christians proclaim that Jesus is the only one through whom anyone can be justified. It is only by virtue of his *divinity* that this consummation can be effected.

According to theists, it would seem, God works within us so that we might recover from our falls. Any simple decision in this life that says *no* to God weakens our Faith and reveals its incompleteness. A free choice action that says *yes* strengthens our Faith and reveals its promise.

We cooperate intimately with God in the process of redemption and recovery. God's justice requires our wholehearted response to saving grace. God does not paint over flaws that remain underneath. God justifies by way of infinite power and infinite love.

Nevertheless, along with God's *infinite* activity, justification can *only* come through our own *willingness to receive* the wholeness that will be effected by this healing infinity—*however painful the experience might have to be.*

A good parent allows a small child to experience the consequences of right and wrong choices in an environment of unconditional love. Much "more so" is the infinitely unconditional love of God allowing us a learning experience, as we grow in truth and love. Thereby we become ready—as a friend, justified forever—to enter freely and worthily the immediate presence of divine Friendship.

God's redemptive Love opens the gates of heaven, but does not push us through. If we are to be justified and enabled to enter this intimately free and perfect love forever, we must also *receive* the processes of rehabilitation and growth. Purgation and sanctification are crucial.

If, indeed, I said *maybe* in the beginning, I am faced with a process of recovery from this incomprehensible pride—a recovery, taking place in this spatiotemporal life, and perhaps, proportionately, in the afterlife. Authentic recovery is never a cover-up. An "easy life" here could only delay, if not make impossible, my purging recovery.

I have to go through "unfair" misfortunes now, in order to move worthily into the radiant splendor of God's presence and love. Once I realize this requirement of justice—as difficult as it might be— then, perhaps, my question about fairness, "Why me?" will become, in all justice *and mercy*, "Why not me?"

Why *Not* Me?

Apparently, Job did not think to ask this question. For the most part, the Jewish, Christian, and Muslim traditions might seem to have avoided it systematically. It seems to suggest masochism.

Rare individuals, however, have learned to *receive* the question. In the predawn blackness of June 5, 2001, Cindi Broaddus experienced her own personal "9/11." As she and her friend drove under an Oklahoma freeway overpass, a jar of acid suddenly crashed through the windshield and burned them. Cindi was *impacted with* a nearly death-dealing affliction. After the most excruciatingly painful kinds of treatment and massive skin grafting during many months, she survived to tell her heroic story to millions on the *Dr. Phil Show*, the *Hour of Power* from the Crystal Cathedral, and on other programs. Her courageous faith in God's goodness, as well as her love for family, friends, neighbors, strangers, and for the unknown assailant, testify to the bountiful potential of the human spirit.

Cindi endured trauma after trauma, physically and emotionally, coming to a spiritual pitch when she broke away from hating another person and what he had done to her. She did a turnaround on herself and realized she hated the person *she had become* in asking, "Why me?" She faced the question head on, "Why *not* me?" She began to hate what she had *allowed* her physical, emotional, and social hurts to do to *her*.

The story of Cindi is told in her compelling book, *A Random Act*. Through her meaningful reflections and ideas, she has stimulated the social movement of 'committing random acts of kindness.' She hopes that, along with millions of others, perhaps her assailant will one day be a recipient of such acts. A random act of violence done to her has occasioned, but not caused, the spreading message of people doing random acts of kindness every day. The specific cause comes from the heart of a beautiful woman.

Along with Cindi and others like her, many of us are strongly inclined to affirm gratefully the goodness that we do find within the world. Then we try to cling in fidelity to the one true God, *despite* our confusion over why bad things happen to good people.

Even the Christian Gospel, with its emphasis on love for God and neighbor through the power of Jesus, presents an apparent problem about both questions: "Why me?" and "Why not me?" Jesus did seem to avoid them.

He was once asked about a man born blind. "Who hath sinned, this man, or his parents, that he should be born blind?" Jesus understood the question to be about personal sin in this world. So, he replied that neither had sinned, but that the blindness was an occasion for the glory of God to be revealed in the healing of the man's sight that he was about to accomplish (*John* 9:1-7).

Jesus could have said more about the problem and the mystery of suffering. But he seemed to be responding to the question as it was asked. Explanation was not his intention. Although he was willing to cite sin as a cause of infirmity, for him the point at issue was the healing power of God, not who sinned when.

In other contexts, however, he left no doubt that *all are sinners*, and that this world, in all its ways, is *subject to the power of Satan, the prince of darkness*.

Someone once questioned him about Galileans whose blood Pilate had shed. Jesus countered with the thought that those who were martyred were not guiltier than anyone else, including those who were asking the question (*Luke* 13:1-5). He referred them to the tower of Siloam falling on people. He said that unless you (askers of such questions) repent and reform your lives, you will all likewise (justly) perish.

The impact is that all have sinned—even children—not just those who were martyred or those on whom the tower fell, and that the misfortunes of these people were not due to any particular sins in *this* life. The principal disaster in Jesus' mind had to be everlasting destruction of anyone's destiny—perishing physically, emotionally, mentally, *and spiritually*.

Suffering is justly related to personal sin. Jesus did not explain how, but he implied this connection. He made oblique reference to it, as when he spoke to a man whom he had just cured at the pool of Bethsaida. The man had been paralyzed for thirty-eight years. Jesus told him that he was now made whole, but that he should sin no more, *lest something worse happen to him* (*John* 5:1-9).

The healer of Galilee left philosophical and theological elucidation to others. The light of Faith-and-love was his concern. What does it matter whether we "gain the whole world" by achieving a rather comprehensive grasp of how sin originally occurred, if we do not repent and become engaged in the submission of our whole being to the holiness of God?

Chapter 10

Another Way of Seeing

In Adam we all sinned.

This poignant claim seems to be made in the Christian Testament (*Romans* 5:12,19). But *how* did that sin occur? Was it *our* sin? Or was it really done only by Adam and Eve?

Did we sin personally *with* Adam immediately upon being created "out of nothing" *and also after* Adam in the history of the world during our lifetime? Or did we sin, as long-standing theologies have apparently taught us, *only* in space and time after Adam?

If our sinning was not done *somehow* personally *with* Adam, how could it be *our sin* at all? Surely, we unique person-creatures of God cannot be *merely* "socially responsible." We must be *personally* responsible for *any* sin that is truly *ours* and that embodies such devastating effects—even if regarded as existing only from the time of conception.

Theists who are alert to the call for vitality in Faith and reason ought to be haunted by the need for a *new way of seeing* some of the basic truths of Revelation. But there is a classic intellective lethargy and defensiveness that are prime products of the ontological gravity of ex-istence, first caused by the *originative* sin that is being denied.

Most theologians, pastors, and good-hearted believers still seem to think that it is *only* or *chiefly* because of *Adam's* sin that we have to endure the sinful world we are now experiencing. They interpret Adam-and-us—our community in and with Adam—in accord with a common mind-set of personal passivity. They would seem to be saying, "How could I, *as I,* be personally involved with such a distant historical progenitor?"

Besides, many theists—devout believers in Islam, for instance—do not believe in an inheritance of Adam's sin. Yet they are still faced with explaining why we are created in the line of Adam and Eve at all, and why every human person does not begin life on the proverbial "level playing field."

The Challenge of Reinterpretation

The standard Christian interpretation has been something like this. After the creation of angels, God decided to create not only angelic creatures, but also humans. So, God created the material universe step by step—whether quickly or not—building up to the creation of man and woman. These two physical humans were partly spiritual—like the angels in being spiritual—having some kind of everlasting destiny.

But then God tested these new creatures in a way proper to them, just as the angels were tested in a manner quite suitable to a purely spiritual response. And, even as many angels failed the challenge and thereby became God's enemies, so the "first humans," Adam and Eve, failed their particular trial and then were driven from their "ideal home."

As a result, we members of the human family inherited their sinful condition. If we were to come into existence at all, we had to be born or conceived, as all human beings are, within the conditions of our first parents. (No difference is recognized between coming into *existence* and coming to *be*.)

This way of generalizing the Revelation is true as far as it goes. It assumes, however, that God is *not necessarily* the Creator of perfect creatures—and that we humans are *not necessarily free* to be, from the start, who we are *willing* to be. We are regarded as being, at first, something like members of a tribal community, and ultimately as laboring necessarily under the myriad subrational constraints of the cosmos.

With regard to the initial conditions for our acting, we are taken to be like members of an animal species: we are stuck with whatever conditions for acting are "handed down" to us through generation.

Under this way of interpreting our origins, we seem to have had no *first* choice about the primal condition of our *being*. We had to be conceived within the natural spiritual damages created by our Goddesignated first parents, Adam and Eve. Our destiny seems to be hazardous and a condition that is forced upon us.

The sin committed at the opening of human history might indeed be the *personal* sin of our first parents and not ours. But is that as far as the truth goes? Hardly. Much more could be said.

If we all die in Adam, as the apostle Paul says (1 *Corinth* 15:22), then we and Adam might have something more in common: a shared responsibility. If so, there is more to this story than the fact of our being created as someone's children: either unwittingly inheriting Adam's sin (as interpreted by Christians only) or entering into the conditions of alienation and inequity resulting from his sin (as understood by Hebrew, Christian, and Islamic thought).

By using our active intelligence and not only our passive mind, we can come to acknowledge more. We can realize that we could have been created together "out of nothing" and "before" any issue of redemptive duration. We could have been gifted with relationships that were *fully interpersonal*: with God and with one another. Adam and all the rest of us could have *received* our beings *together*. With whole hearts, we could have immediately entered everlasting bliss.

But if we all die in Adam, did we not all stray together with him? And then, as a result, did Adam become first in the parent-child line of redemptive recovery?

In the *originative, personal* sin we, together *with* Adam, first turned away from the Light of God. We and multitudes of others, including Adam, failed, *on our own and together,* to be in the light of our unique be-ings. We *endarkened ourselves and crashed* with him.

Then God drew Adam from the "dust of the earth."

Moreover, when it was "our turn" to *receive conception* within the space-time, rehabilitative world, we became sinners *in* Adam. By virtue of his *historically original* sin, then, we were *identifiable* as sinful.

Nevertheless, crucial to deepening our vision is an understanding of our underlying, ontologically *originative,* sin and its deformative character.

As indicated in Chapter 1, there is something missing in the idea of God *testing* persons created "out of nothing." These beings are presumably "fresh from" God's perfect word *BE*.

Our *first* act of freedom, responding to *this* gift, must have been a free exercise of perfect *active potential* that failed its own perfect, God-given nature. *This* is the act that caused the "cosmess," within which God is now rescuing all of us who are *willing* to be saved.

In our pristine act of freedom, we were at *our untempted best* with perfect freedom to say *yes*. But it was *not* a "test." God's "best" needs no test.

No finite person—whether angelic or human in kind—was subject to a "creation test." We who are already-compromised persons here in the *maybe* world seem compelled to project the idea of a test, gleaned from our world now, onto the originative interactivity of God with perfectly created persons.

But the first act of freedom is *necessarily* untempted and untested. There was no passive potency in the person to be acted upon. And the power to act purely was perfect. Only human persons who partly failed in their first act of freedom—and thereby *caused* their own passivity—had to be "tested": to reveal *to themselves* their own self-contorted condition of *be*-ing.

Our Responsibility within Revelation

The originative creation had to be an *interpersonal act*. God acts only relationally and by sheer personhood. Always Person to person. Never Person to thing, because a thing cannot *personally receive* even its own being, much less God's.

God alone acted. But, since this infinite act was perfectly *bringing persons to be*, these persons were *necessarily intended* in the very act. And their reciprocal activity or response—their own acting—was immediate. There was no duration at all between the gifting act of creating and the responding act of the created ones.

In creating, the *gifting* Person (God) necessarily faced Self (God) with the *gifted* (finite) persons, who necessarily gave fully knowing and willing responses.

God could not have intended subpersonal (imperfect) creatures in *that* creation. But we were both the intended gifts and the gifted ones. We obviously failed somewhat in our immediate response. We did not fulfill our response-*ability*.

Our failure was unique. We were not tempted. And we did not "choose" from a set of alternatives already present. Immediately *out of the insuperable gift* that is our *being*, we freely created a defective personal response.

Our consciousness at that primal moment was—compared to our level of consciousness in the present world—a super-consciousness. Our powers to know and to love were simply perfect. But our first *act* of willing with these perfect powers must have been, at least ever so slightly, self-warped.

Similarly, *now* we struggle to awaken from the resultant crash and to participate in recovery, within the *redemptive* creation. Besides, we are also failing somewhat in our response to divine *Revelation*— revelation *about* this creation of recovery.

Revelation, like creation, is an *interpersonal act* on God's part. But what about *our* part? Are we responding by taking an active part in Revelation—our part in *the very act of communication*? "Even for God" communication is a "two way street."

Genesis and the other Sacred Scriptures tell us much about God's rescue operation, but not so much about *why* it was needed in the first place. Perhaps that is because the *answer* to the question *why* ought to come *strictly from us*, who are *solely* responsible *for* it. God is responsible for the efficacy of the redemptive activity and for its Revelation. But *we*—not God—have been responsible for *why* it was required.

Perhaps we are being called to admit—*on our own*—that we are *essentially* and *personally* responsible for *needing* to be redeemed, recovered, and saved. Maybe we are now being challenged to drop our passive instinct to excuse ourselves and to blame "the big three," Adam and Eve and Satan. Perhaps we ought to stop making excuses for ourselves by saying, for instance, that there is nothing *revealed* in the Bible concerning an *originative* sin.

We might even come to admit that such a primal sin could have been hidden from us by the writers of the Sacred Scriptures—and hidden from themselves by themselves. This truth of the personal, originative sin could be so immediate and overwhelming that we cannot "see" it. We could be looking right at it, but really failing to apprehend it. And the sacred writers could be revealing it without knowing that they are doing so.

Moreover, this aspect of revelation might not be a fitting subject for *reportorial* Revelation, including the Scriptural. The content of Revelation that is reported includes such events and conditions as the creation of the world of space and time, the fall, our sinfulness, the historical redemption, and our personal need for salvation. These are critically needed orientations and facts.

Grant, at least for the moment, that originative sin is real and that it came from our first free act of be-ing. Could it then be merely reported? Would not revelation of such a sin have to be specifically *self*-revelational. This self-revelation might be part of the required context for fully appreciating the necessary reportorial content of Revelation about our salvation.

Originative sin would *not* be a "new revelation" of content, but a new depth in apprehending the essentials. And this sin would not be *reported* so much as *admitted*. We are being called to *respond*, while participating in a powerful paradox.

On the one hand, a personal and communal originative sin needs no further revelation than what we already know and believe. People can be saved without knowing about originative sin *explicitly*. We can admit to being sinful and being in dire need of salvation. We do not have to realize the magnitude of the sin any more than we realize the magnitude of our heavenly destiny once we repent.

On the other hand, the more explicit we can make the authentic grounds for believing in the necessity of repentance and personal salvation, the more likely it is that people can be converted. So, it is urgent to attempt to ferret out reasons for "the human predicament." The deeper our acknowledgement before God and one another, the *more effectively* the truth of sin and salvation can be *lived*.

An admission of our radical personal failing, right at the moment of creation *ex nihilo* ("out of nothing"), would further the meaning of creation in *Genesis.* That latter meaning has emphatically spread among the peoples of the world over many hundreds of years. But it begs deeper and richer sustenance.

Perhaps the time has finally come—within a world attuned to the massive powers of *emotional* repression—to recognize the *spiritual* power to repress. We must come to admit our unprecedented ability to cover over the ultimate origin of human evil, done at the moment of originative creation.

In order to do this, we would require another way of seeing—of seeing "what we have been looking at." We might come to know that in the heart of creation—deeper than the story of Adam and Eve—there is the virtually untold story of *our first freedom.*

The present volume attempts to put us in touch with that crucial story, so long-repressed within the human heart. This effort is not a Gnostic endeavor, but an up-front exercise of human reason working beingfully (ontologically) within the received truth of Revelation, quite accessible to all.

The benefits of bringing an absolutely originative sin into personal consciousness might be considerable.

We might gain insight, for instance, by making a serious attempt to know our critical need for *spiritual* healing. The truth heals and sets us free in spiritual healing—far more than in emotional healing. The power for the healing that is common to both the emotional and the spiritual, would be the *light of truth.*

In emotional matters of repression, we have learned how important it is to allow the light of one's own mind to play upon the truth. The light of the mind itself can be healing, if we would only induce exposure.

For instance, latent feelings of resenting, or desiring, someone will remain repressed until courageous activities are undertaken. The emotionally charged person, for instance, by genuinely therapeutic means, turns the light of his or her consciousness to the possibility or plausibility that such repression is occurring.

Similarly, we can come to affirm that some awesome truths and their implications need to surface within our *spiritual* lives. Keeping truth repressed and shutting out the light will impede our repentance and reinforce our brokenness.

We are hurting ourselves by not being willing to give God *all the glory of the Immaculate Creation*. The idea that God *could* have initially created us as merely good and not perfectly good reveals an appalling insensitivity to the divine power and goodness. The divine activity of creating was an absolutely infinite activity in which every human person was gifted freely and perfectly by the heart of God. You and I were among them.

At the beginning of the new millennium, we can now join with others in deepening our sense *both* of God's infinite intimacy in creating *and* of our personal originative sin *against* divine intimacy that left us with a being-searing need for repentance.

In matters of *spiritual* repression, we need to acknowledge the truth and bring it to the *light of communal consciousness*. We can let ourselves admit the in-depth reality of personal sinfulness. And we are called to bring originative sin prayerfully into the light of the Holy Spirit of God. That task is, at least, partly and critically *ours*.

Then we might come to know new depths of repentant joy and new levels of meaning for our relationships with God and with one another.

Carrying the Cross of Paradox

Our functional inability or unwillingness to see our own creational sin constitutes an ongoing disaster. Our intransigence has crippled the meanings for creation and for freedom in the great traditions of theism.

We freely failed to confirm for ourselves, at the absolute moment of creation, the perfect being that we were given. The repercussions of that miscarriage of freedom—as well as of its cover-up—now *unconsciously* perpetrate intense opposition to any of our efforts to *admit* the radical depths of our structural and spiritual diminishment. We hold ourselves in a colossal bind—a spiritual repression.

We are challenged to reach into our power to understand reality as paradox. We must be willing to acknowledge the *both-and* character of the truths that we contemplate.

For instance, Adam and Eve *both* are *and* are not the exclusive originators of human evil. *They are the originators of the familial procession of human evil that comes into space, time, and history. But they are not, and cannot be, the originators of the evil that comes from each of us and constitutes our predicament as fallen humans in need of being conceived in the world of redemption—the world of space and time.*

Failure to distinguish adequately between the temporal and the everlasting dimensions of freedom inclines us to be blind to what is happening even in the sensible world. We can overlook important distinctions that lead us to a better understanding of ourselves.

In considering how evil came into this world, we must sharpen our focus. Human persons come *from*—in the sense of "out of"—*neither* God *nor* their parents.

Human beings come into being-at-all *by* the infinitely powerful, good, and free activity of God, *in and out of* nothing. They come into being and into being-themselves in perfect freedom.

But those who become children in space and time—as essentially persons, and fully, though not exclusively, spiritual beings—are already-comatose humans. Such persons come into *this* world—by the redemptive, remedial activity of God—only *from and out of themselves* and from their gravely impaired beings. They do so, of course, *with* and *through* other humans, including their immediate parents, their most remote parents, Adam and Eve, and countless other parents in between.

From their parents, children inherit possessions of all sorts, as well as genetic dispositions toward physical makeup and psychological predilections toward traits of character. They might even inherit propensities toward spiritual strengths and weaknesses.

But we ought to acknowledge that even *physical* inheritance is *essentially indirect*: the child does not "have" his father's and his mother's genetic endowments. The child has only his or her own. Half of the child's unique genes have been *caused specifically by* the father's genes carried within a particular sperm cell and half by the mother's genes carried within a particular ovum.

But it is false, and dreadfully misleading, to think that inheritance means the parents "pass on" their very own genes to the children, as they might pass family heirlooms. Only a sluggish consciousness is satisfied with seeing it that way.

The whole body of the child, as well as the psyche and spirit, is the *child's*. It does not belong to the parents' bodies—not even in part. Our careless consciousness impedes vision. We are quite inclined to confuse likeness with partial identity.

For instance, when we speak of "identical twins" we really know that there is no such thing. Identical would mean that the one is the same as the other or that they are interchangeable. Nevertheless, no matter how much the two *look* alike, each one is *unique* in *being*. So, too, there is not the slightest partial identity between parent and child. It only looks that way.

We are easily misled. Even in the biological sciences, we speak as though the sperm and ovum, the parental gametic cells, *unite* to form the zygote. But we are quite deceived by appearances—even under a microscope. These two causative cells dynamically *interact* and *die* together in the formation of the unique zygotic cell that constitutes *bodily* the spatiotemporal existence of the completely new person (or persons).

The offspring might look as though they physically "spring off" the parents—as though they were almost literally "chips off the old block." That, however, is only because our consciousness is not sufficiently attuned to giving every *be*-ing its due.

We do not come *from* the substances of our parents, but *through* the mediation of their substances. We come *from the ontologically comatose substance of ourselves.*

On reflection, we can come to realize that the sperm and ovum are two "part-body" cells, and not "whole-body" cells. As cells, sperm and ovum are simply *parts* of the *parents'* bodies. Together these cells *cause* the baby's existence *in space and time*. Nevertheless, they are not, and can never become, a "whole-body cell"—which is exactly what the new bodily being is as a zygote. The *energy* of the zygote includes the brain, heart, and all the organs of the individual that later develop physically. Moreover, *all* human energy (the effect of fractuation) is spiritually caused—including both the physical and the emotional. Our brain and the other organs were *naturally* there in existence when we were zygotes, but were not *functional* yet.

You and I were once zygotes. But we were never—nor could be ever—a sperm or an ovum, each of which is, essentially and always, as such, a *part* of the father or mother, respectively.

It is curious how mindless we can be in our thought and speech—even at professional levels. We ought only to say that the sperm and ovum *unite* to form a zygote in the same way we say that the sun *rose* this morning: namely, figuratively. Actually, the sun has never "risen" in the geophysical history of the universe. It has only "risen" in the sluggish, egocentric consciousness of folks like you and me.

Similarly, a sperm and an ovum have never actually *united* to form a zygote within the biologic history of the whole world. Their nuclei dynamically interact and die together in the process of *co-causing* the zygote. *Through* their causality an already existent, ontologically comatose person begins to root within the explicitly spatiotemporal world.

Only when we come to take *being* more seriously—the *being* of things, the *being* of actions, and the *being* of people—will we be able to get a theological breakthrough in understanding our origins at physical, emotional, and spiritual levels.

Our egocentric, "either-or" mentality must yield to our capacity to think and speak, as well, from the potentiality of our "both-and" mentality. And this latter "mind spring" is at the roots of our being.

Putting it into practice, we can say that everyone has the potential for the two mentalities. Both abilities are good and necessary: to evaluate things as *either* right *or* wrong, *either* good *or* bad, as well as to recognize actions and situations that are *both* good *and* bad.

The either-or mentality, for instance, enables us to recognize the principle of non-contradiction: that a thing cannot be and not be at the same time and in the same respect. I cannot be both a child and not a child on September 30, 1945 with respect to bodily maturity. Correlatively, the both-and mentality makes it possible to see that I can both be and not be a child even today with respect to my attitude toward God and my physiological age. That is, I can be both a child (spiritually) and not a child (physiologically).

Adam and Eve can be said, therefore, *both* to be *and* not to be the origin of sin within our lives. They are the origin in the line of time. They are the origin historically and cosmically, and perhaps in other ways as well. But they are *not the origin* in *be*-ing.

Every personal being *as a being* is "face to Face" with God. Any other being that serves as a mediator or mediating influence does so only in the midst of our heart-to-Heart relationship with our Creator. In *that* relationship, we create our response to the total gift of be-ing and to God's infinitely giving love.

Our May-be-ing

So, we have engaged in our incipient, perfectly free response. Paradoxically, this reply to *being* turned out to be quite an imperfect one. The freedom *power* was perfect. But our freedom *act*—done by *us* with that *power*—was imperfect. Right now we are suffering the structurally internal and external consequences of that originative act of response to *be*-ing.

About our prospects for being saved and prepared for everlasting life we can be *both* hopeful *and* disheartened. Quite hopeful in view of the *infinite* compassion, love, and power of God. Yet somewhat disheartened because of our original *and continuing* acts of willing rather badly concerning what is before us.

If Faith means anything at all, it means we have to put all our trust in God, and *ultimately* no *definitive* trust in ourselves or in other sinful creatures. To trust in God *is* to trust authentically in oneself. Not to trust in God is not to *trust* in self, but to "hold tight" to self. We absolutely *need* God to effect our redemption and salvation from the originative crash.

Paradoxically, this personal recovery can be *accomplished* only by acknowledging our utter *inability* to do it at all *by ourselves*. Yet, in order to be *saved* by God, *we* are called to offer our *willingness*— our sincere and honest, wholehearted *yes*—to God *and also* to our being, just as it is, even now, in the misery of sinfulness.

Right from the word—God's word—*BE*, we responded *may*-be. And we are now *be*-ing that response. We are not so much *be-ing* as *may-be-ing*.

Our *may-be-ing* should reveal to us that our absolute creation was interpersonal and that it was an inter-freedom activity. Our perfect, gifted freedom interacted with God's infinite freedom. God did not "freely impose" any *passivity* upon our gifted be-ing. We did. We received immediately and freely our being and our being-this-self in a less than perfectly responsive manner.

That failure caused or created *ex aliquo*—*out of* this pure gift, *by* this gift itself—a reticence to be and to be fully who we are. We are alienated from our essence right within it.

Traditionally, our essence has been portrayed as passive potency in relation to the *act* of be-ing. But that is not essence *as God gifted us*. That is essence as our less-than-fully receptive self *made itself to be*.

By my failure in signature freedom, *what I am* is not fully *who I am*. *What I am* is the kind of being that can be *done to*—that can be *acted upon*, rather than simply be *interacted with*. Such is the self-constituted part of my be-ing: I am the kind of be-ing that is *may*-be-ing, arrogantly giving "permission" to God to "work on me." I lack a simplicity of being to ask myself to "work *with* God" for salvation.

As a result of our common predicament of being—unique persons meagerly relating with God and with one another—we are called to *let in* the new light shed by the supposition of our being personally and ultimately responsible for the origin of good-and-evil in our lives. The original sin of Adam and Eve can then be accorded a less prominent, but significant place in the history of our attempts at recovery. Blaming our first parents for our being-here holds some critically important truth, but not the prime truth about origins.

By implicitly, yet inevitably, blaming God for allowing us to be conceived in this broken world—a world that we supposedly had nothing at all to do with starting—we amazingly ignore the *infinity* of divine Goodness and disparage the *infinity* of divine Power.

But, then, that is just what a distortion of *first freedom* would have done. By failing to admit our essentially personal responsibility for our defectively limited life in this world, we are being *consistent* with that quite original act of *self*-deception. We are not consciously acknowledging our immediate act of interpersonally responding to the gift of being-at-all.

We might admit consciously that our creation was an interpersonal act. Or we might unconsciously overlook it. In any event, we are going to give an interpersonal response at death. Jesus told us what he as God would say to us, depending on the character of our love in this purgative world. He will say, "Come to me…" or "Depart from me…" And how well we have been *loving* here will turn out to be our ringing, everlasting *yes* or *no* to Love Eternal. We will be saying *yes* or *no* to being repentant for our originative *maybe*.

About the Author

Robert E. Joyce is *professor emeritus* of philosophy at St. John's University in Minnesota. He received a B.A. in philosophy from the University of St. Mary of the Lake, Mundelein, Illinois, 1957; an M.A. in philosophy from De Paul University, 1960; and a Ph.D. in philosophy from International College, 1978. The doctoral courses of study were completed at the University of Notre Dame, 1959-61. At Notre Dame, he maintained a Teaching Fellowship, 1959-61, and was appointed instructor of philosophy, 1961-62. He has taught courses at De Paul University, Loyola University, and the College of St. Benedict. His principal teaching has been done at St. John's University, 1962-94. At St. John's, for several years he served as Director of the Tri-College Honors Program and for several years as Chair of the Philosophy Departments at St. John's and the College of St. Benedict.

Dr. Joyce is the author of various books and numerous articles in scholarly and popular publications. He published with Mary Rosera Joyce, his wife, the first pro-life paperback in the United States, *Let Us Be Born: The Inhumanity of Abortion* (Chicago: Franciscan Herald Press, 1970). In the same year, Mary and Robert published their unique introduction to the philosophy of man and woman, *New Dynamics in Sexual Love: A Revolutionary Approach to Marriage and Celibacy* (Collegeville, MN: St. John's University Press, 1970). Sections of Robert's doctoral dissertation, *Human Sexual Ecology: A Philosophy and Ethics of Man and Woman* (University Press of America, 1981), has been used in University courses and by several leaders in the natural family planning movement.

Meeting the Challenge Posed by the Perennial Conflation of Creations

In other books (see final page), such as *A Perfect Creation: The Light behind the Dark Side of Genesis* (LifeCom, 2008) and *Affirming Our Freedom in God: The Untold Story of Creation* (LifeCom, 2001), I attempt to develop a beginning ontology of creation, highlighting creation *ex nihilo* as a necessarily interpersonal act of giving and receiving being. Discussed are some of the major ontological features and consequences that such an understanding yields.

I am interested in gaining various responses to the new perspective that is briefly introduced in those books and in the present book, *God Said, We Said*. This book is the first in a trilogy that is called *When God Said Be, We Said Maybe: An Inside Story of the Creation, the Crash, and the Recovery of Being*.

The ideas in this first book are considerably developed in the following volumes, *God Says, We Say: The Interpersonal Act of Redemption*, and *God Will Say, We Will Say: The Interpersonal Act of Salvation*.

On behalf of this project, any observations, suggestions, or objections will be afforded careful attention. Also, any suggested relevant material would be welcome.

I also encourage dialog by email.

Robert E. Joyce, Ph.D.
Professor Emeritus
St. John's University
Collegeville, Minnesota

Phone   320-252-9866
email   robertjoyce@charter.net
Website www.Lifemeaning.com

Works Cited

Armstrong, Karen. *A History of God*: *The 4,000-Year Quest of Judaism, Christianity and Islam.* New York: Ballantine, 1994.

Bible. The Holy Bible, Douay Version.

Biebel, David B. *If God Is So Good, Why Do I Hurt So Bad?* Grand Rapids, Mich.: Baker Publishing Group, 1995.

Blumenthal, David. *Facing the Abusing God*: *A Theology of Protest.* Louisville, Ky.: Westminster John Knox Press, 1993.

Broaddus, Cindi, with Kimberly Lohman Suiters. *A Random Act.* New York: HarperCollins, 2005.

Chopra, Deepak. *How to Know God*: *The Soul's Journey into the Mystery of Mysteries.* New York: Harmony Books, 2000.

Krauss, Pesach, and Morrie Goldfischer. *Why Me? Coping with Grief, Loss, and Change.* New York: Bantam Books, 1990.

Kushner, Harold. *When Bad Things Happen to Good People.* New York: Avon, 1981.

Quran. The Holy Quran, paraphrased from multiple sources.

Wiesel, Elie. *Night.* Westminster, Md.: Bantam Dell, 1982.

Glossary

The new theistic view requires an adventure in revisiting traditional terms. Faith and reason need an increase in depth-perspective on perennial truths.

Painters, for instance, once rendered their images in largely flat, 2-dimensional presentations. They seemed to be incapable of knowing how to represent the third dimension successfully. Similarly, because of a cosmological crunch, traditional philosophy and theology tend to be 2-dimensional in presenting the great truths. If possible, our effort here is to change *not the truths, but the perspective* for the sake of better vision.

The following definitions and delineations of key terms might assist the reader's thinking about prospects for a better theistic view. These words and phrases are analogical, not univocal. They do not have one single, exclusive meaning. For brevity and practicality, however, only one or two main meanings are set down for each term.

Some of the following terms are not used in this particular book, but might serve to fill out the perspective for readers interested in philosophical and theological "details." The Glossary may be read in itself as a review.

Being and Becoming

Being (*ens*) can mean the totality of a given being: who or what it is. But, more specifically, be-ing (*esse*) is the *act*uality of being-at-all. Be-ing is the most important *act* of a whole being. All other acts and actualities, such as thinking, drinking, walking, talking, *et al.* are "branches of the act of be-ing." Somewhat counter to the traditional theism, being is regarded, in this book, as what we *are* and *do*. Be-ing is the gift God gives us to *be* and to *do*. We do our being. God does not. Being is an act, not merely a fact.

We do not simply "have" being. We *are* the entire be-ing God gifted us uniquely to *be* and to *do*. No part of our being is *of* God or *of* anyone else. We are fully and forever our own unique being, thanks to the *infinitely* powerful gifting of God.

Only persons are *whole* (complete) beings. Subpersonal beings (from molecules to monkeys) are *part* (incomplete) beings. They cannot receive themselves within themselves and so are not, and *cannot be, fully* what they are. (See *excidents.*)

To *be* is to be *unique* (to be not the same as anything else) *and* to be *uniquely related* (to every other being that is). For person-beings, to *be* is (also) to *be-with*.

Existence is a *way* of being, of standing outside of self and other things. *Ex-sistere* means to "stand out of." But God and all created persons who said fully *yes* to creation *ex nihilo* do not *exist*; they simply *are*. They have no passivity to "overcome" by striving to get out of or go beyond their condition of being.

All material beings, as we know them now, not only *are*, but *ex-ist*. Subpersonal beings exist by having "parts outside of parts," by being extended, material realities. Personal beings who, like us, have fallen—who are defective—*ex-ist* also by reflective consciousness, whereby they "stand outside" themselves by being conscious of themselves, the better to direct themselves and make choices (the existentialist aspect).

Failure to distinguish meaningfully between *being* and *existence* (in any language equivalent) can be seen as a particularly instructive sign of our originative repression of our *first* act of *be*-ing and of the ex-istence that this act caused.

The *pre-conceptive latency of our fallen being* (*ontological latency*) is the coma-like, disordered way of being from which we emerge at conception. It was caused immediately by the crash of saying *maybe* at the moment of creation *ex nihilo*.

This condition of collapsed being before existence (conception) has nothing to do with reincarnation or even incarnation. There was no "taking on" of any kind. The perfect (finite) ontological structure with which we were gifted at creation *ex nihilo* was compromised by our imperfect response. Immediately, we became imperfect created persons by way of *adding* an *imperfect receiving* to our originative perfection or giftedness. We became, as it were, "bloated in our being." Our perfect, God-gifted essence remained, but our nature—the disposition to act according to essence—was self-distorted.

Maybe-sayers thus subsist prior to their ex-istence in space and time at conception. Our pre-conceptive latency results from the condition of our being following the moment of *our imperfect response* given to originative creation right up to the moment of conception. Our self-conflicted be-ing (including powers to know and love) was relatively dysfunctional until that event. We were not fallen angels, but simply fallen humans.

Energy is the natural capacity to work: to struggle, strain, move forward, exercise potencies to do and to be done to. It arises from the fractuation (fractured actuation) done by the *maybe*-saying of originatively sinning persons and it comes in many forms at various levels of redemptive causality. Without any originative sin, there would be no need or occasion for energy. Every reality would be itself a *pure act* or *actuality*—whether infinite or finite. No work to be done. Simply, the play of everlasting life.

Essence is *what* someone or something *is*. While one can focus on the essences of qualities and activities of entities, the prime signification relates to the *fundamental what*: *what* is a person, *what* is this thing or that thing as such. Fundamentally, what *kind* of person or thing is this as different from other kinds of reality?

But there are really two different—almost always confused—kinds of essence: *common* (e.g., human) and *individual* (e.g., *this* human). The confusion between, say, the humanness and Jamesness of James makes for much metaphysical mischief in giving an account of being *as being*. *What James is* as this unique human (his uniqueness of person) is not at all the same as his being a human kind of being.

Nature is the essence of someone or something as this essence is disposed to act. What kinds of activity can be expected from a particular entity? Granted the essence of a peach tree is to produce peaches—not apples, oranges, *et al.*—its nature is the inexorable disposition to do just that. The way the being expresses itself, or can express itself, in action is its nature. *Nature* is, so to say, *how* the *essence* can reveal itself in acting. In saying *maybe* to being and God, the *self acts through* its essence, but *in and by* its nature.

Form (substantial form), traditionally conceived, is that principle in the essence of a person or thing *by which* the entity is *fundamentally what* it is. It is an intrinsic *part* of the essence. All things have substantial forms: one for each kind of thing.

This traditional meaning is considerably modified by the theses of this book. In the new view, substantial form is the principle of the person (not of things) *by which* he or she is able to give self to self and to all others as a principle of essence. In the new view, it is called "givity": the capacity specifically to give in a receiving way. It is the principle that is co-active with matter and is a dimension of the *act* of *be*-ing. To be is to be giftive (and to be receptive).

In the new view, human *souls* are the substantial forms *as they serve* human persons in their recovering from defective exercise of "givity" at the moment of their originative creation. Souls as (reparative) substantial forms serve fallen humans in their struggle to attain the pristine, God-intended condition of gifting selves fully at the moment of creation.

Matter (prime matter), traditionally conceived, is that principle in the essence of a human person or of a thing *out of which* the entity is *fundamentally what* it is. Matter is an intrinsic part of the essence. All things in matter and motion, space and time, involve prime matter, from which every diverse kind of thing is developed. It is the ultimately common feature of substances in the cosmos. None can exist without it. This traditional meaning has been, however, considerably modified—not negated—by the theses of this book.

Prime matter (reconceived in the super-light of Faith and of ontological reflection), first of all, is the principle of the human *person* (not of any *thing*) *by which* he or she is able to receive self from within self as a characteristic of essence. (Angels have no prime matter. Their kind of essence itself is pure receptivity to their be-ing.) (God's Being is pure *infinite* receptivity, as well as infinite givity.) This pure receptivity-power, co-constitutive of the essence, was gifted at the moment of creation *ex nihilo*.

In the new view, matter is a kind of *receptivity*: the capacity to *receive* one's essence in a giving way—and not at all "to be done to" or "to be determined." The prime matter and substantial form are totally correlative as the roots of all receiving and giving in the human person from the moment of originative creation.

Originative matter was *purely* **active receptivity**—*the active power or potency to receive who and what* we are. It was not—originatively—the *passivity* or passive receptivity delineated by Aristotle.

Pure originative receiving is actually as active and real as giving. *Originatively*, there is no passivity.

With our bad originative response, prime matter as sheer receptivity within our essence had to begin functioning as prime matter that is passive, a capacity to "be done to" right within the essence and to function in common with the extrinsic energy of subpersonal creation. Out of this passive condition, human bodies were formed. Our bodies are prime matter *as it serves* human persons in attempting to attain the pristine condition of receptivity intended by God at the moment of creation.

Angelic persons, however, in their greater simplicity and likeness to God's infinite receptivity, are without this co-principle within their essence. Originatively, angels are simple, sheer receptivities for the act of be-ing.

Soul and Body are terms we use unconsciously, for the most part, to indicate the form and matter principles of human essence in their self-weakened condition. By these principles of becoming, we humans grope for salvation. Soul and body, however, are distinct from the originative **form** and **matter** that are purely active.

In the tradition, the soul is the principle of life in that which has life and comes from Aristotle's philosophy of nature. The body is the "stuff" of matter that the form specifically determines. The body is 'supinely' related to form as to its virtually sole principle of intelligibility. This manner of conceiving represents the unawareness in the tradition of an originative sin that has passivized both form and matter into the conditions of crash and hopeful recovery now recognized as soul and body.

The following terms—except purely active potency—apply strictly to existents in the cosmos, not to angelic creatures.

Substance is, above all, quite like what Aristotle said it was in the first instance (primary substance): this whole being…its essence, with all its attributes and weaknesses, concretely and singly. More specifically, in accord with the common tradition, substance (second substance) is also that principle in the being of a person or thing *by which* the entity is or exists *in and through itself* and not in and through any other. Every created substance is its own principle of intrinsic being and activity (but not its own ultimate cause). It remains the source of natural stability in the midst of accident-modifications or changes. In space and time, substance relates to accidents as passive potency (*q.v.*), out of which qualities and acts develop.

Accidents are not the substance, but parts of the substance, through which the substance *manifests itself.* An accident, such as the color of a tree or the thought of a human, does not be or exist in and through itself, but only *in and through another* (a substance). The act of walking and even the power to walk, as instances, are accidents and cannot be or exist "on their own" or in and through themselves. There is no act of walking without a walker, nor act of thinking without a thinker. Yet the acts are real; they express or manifest the substance or the agent; they are never discounted —even if minor.

Excidents, according to the new theistic view, are the super-multiplicity of substances and their accidents in the cosmos that are not *entitatively* human. Excidents are *everything in the whole of space and time*, including every particle of organic and inorganic matter—and excluding human substance (persons) with all their accidents. At the base of all excidents lies the supremely low level of human (non-entitative) fallen freedom that empowers the telic character of all matter and motion. All material things tend, however erratically, to an end or fulfillment of inherent purpose by virtue of their being entities created by God out of fallen human freedom (energy).

At the absolute moment of creation *ex nihilo*, *excidents* resulted from the ontological explosion caused by our immediate response. They are forms of the passive-reactivity (i.e., energy) emanating from the originative sin that was constituted by the first acts of innumerable humans who said *maybe* to their be-ing. These elements of discarded human freedom were separated from malreceptive, freedom-abusive sinning persons themselves. As subpersonal (partial) beings (from molecules to monkeys), they were developed by God's *infinitely* loving activity of compassion on the *maybe*-sayers.

Energy originally emanated from the partial rejection (the fractuality) of perfect personal beings as we were gifted to be. All energy is originatively human energy—frustrated human freedom—and is of two basic kinds: *fragmental* and *non-fragmental*. On the one hand, excidents are *fragmental* energy, "broken off" from the substance of the *maybe*-sayers in and by the ontological "big bang." On the other hand, fallen human substances retained a kind of *non-fragmental* energy that is therapeutic and intrinsic to them. The result is our defective substances ex-isting with their accidents (including bodily life in the cosmos).

Active potency is the ability or capacity to *do* something or to *perform* a certain kind of activity. By creation *ex nihilo* we were gifted to *be* pure active potencies of be-ing—each person fully able both to receive and to give personal be-ing. After originative sin, fallen human being has the active (natural) capacity (whether functional or not) to reason and to love; a dog does not. A dog has the active potency to bark and wag its tail; a human does not. *Pure* active potency, however, is the kind of being we were gifted to be *out of nothing* with the angels. It was not mixed with any passive potency. We created the latter by our less-than-full response.

Passive potency is the ability or capacity to *be done to*, to *be affected by* or determined by someone else or something else. A tree has the capacity (passive potency) to be bent by the wind; a boulder does not. A boulder has the capacity (passive potency) to be rolled down a hill; a (living) tree does not.

Moreover, "prime matter" in the traditional sense is a sheerly passive receptivity—prime passive potency. In the new view, however, prime matter is *originatively* a supreme, purely active, receptivity of essence right within the essence—an *active potency*. God does *not*, and cannot, create *directly* out of nothing any passive potency.

As perfectly self-actuated, angels and saints in heaven are purely active potencies that co-act *with* God and the others, without being acted *upon* or determined in any way. There is no *passive* potency in beatitude.

Creation

Creation *ex nihilo* (out of nothing) is the *originative beginning of all finite being*. God infinitely loved persons into being. In this creation, only persons resulted—out of nothing, and not out of any preceding substance. The creation was immediate, non-durational, and immaculate. Each person was unique and perfect in every way, including the freedom (purely active potency) to say *yes* fully. There was no temptation or ability to *be* tempted. Simply, there was gifted an invitation to *being with* God and all others 'ecstatically' forever.

This creation was perfectly *interpersonal* in divine intent and solely an act of God.

Creation *ex aliquo* (out of something) is the *secondary* or *derivative* act of creation: a creation of *be-coming* or of being coming back to itself from a crash and from its own ontological self-conflict. This remedial act of God began at the same moment as creation *ex nihilo* and our response. God "works with and out of" the results of the originative crash of those persons who said *maybe* to the gift of being at the moment of the *ex nihilo* creation. Infinite love and power interacts with finite, free resistance that is both conscious and unconscious.

This redemptive opportunity for saving these "fallen human persons" is what is directly the subject of *Genesis* and other Scriptures. According to Christian teaching, this redemptive creation of *becoming* culminated in the death and resurrectional life of Jesus Christ. At least, it can be said that, for all three theistic traditions, only God can redeem and save us.

Originative *creation* is interpersonal, yet solely the act of God. But the act of *salvation* itself is more. It is an interpersonal action of finite freedom completely cooperating with infinite freedom.

Immaculate creation is another name for the interpersonal, immediate, durationless originative creation *ex nihilo* by which God gifted into being perfect persons with perfect freedom. Being pure and unique acts of personhood, these persons are able to receive their being perfectly. The result of God's act of creating was beings unstained by any passivity at all. All gifted persons (angelic and human) were purely (immaculately) who and what they were by the power of the infinitely loving heart of God and necessarily gave their interpersonal response (*yes, no,* or *maybe*). The act of angels was either *yes* or *no*. The act of humans was *yes, no,* or *maybe*.

Freedom and Sin

Freedom is the correlative capacity of intellect and will to let the person be present to, and unite with, the Being of God *and* to participate in the fundamental goods of human personhood. Essence-freedom is structured to unite directly with—*not an identity with*—the essence of God, if or when beatitude is attained.

Natural freedom is, then, the *essential disposition* to know and to love, to the fullest extent of one's capacity of be-ing.

Functional freedom is the actual ability to do the knowing and loving. Both natural and functional freedom are gifted in originative creation. But the defective response of the first *act* of our freedom maimed them both, functionally separating them from each other and also from the freedom of essence, the being as originatively gifted.

The alternatives of *yes*, *no*, or *maybe* were not set up "ahead of time." Our originative freedom was "pre-alternative." Before we broke out into the alternative conditions of being-and-becoming, we were—like God—*free* only to say *yes*. But being finite, we were *able* to say *no*. We were not *free* to say *no*; but we were *able* and did, *de facto*—*severely damaging our freedom*. Only with that defective response did there arise the passively based kind of freedom with its alternatives and choices.

Originative sin is our *first maybe* (less than a full *yes*), said to God and ourselves with perfect, untempted freedom, given at the non-durational, immediate moment of creation *ex nihilo*. The degree of *no* in that *maybe* is not the only cause, but it is the ultimate cause, of all evil *in which we find ourselves involved.*

This primal sin caused *our very exposure* to the evils done by others—including the forces of Satan—as well as evils done by ourselves. Without originative sin we would be completely blissful in be-ing. By this abuse of perfect freedom we are now in the cosmic world of space and time—"all spaced out" and "doing time."

Original sin in Eden is a subject for *reportorial* Revelation. It is known by Faith in Scripture and Tradition. *Originative* sin, however, is a subject for our *personal* admission. It was not at all one of our temporal decisions or events, and thereby it could not be readily "reported." But it can be *admitted* in the light of Revelation. This signature sin is surely received unconsciously by Faith in Scripture and Tradition; and it is discerned, at least somewhat, by the awareness of our being as *be*-ing—by beingfully (ontologically) received Faith.

Original sin is the first recorded historical sin. Adam and Eve committed this disobedience as they were tested through the serpent. God "predicted" it in saying that on the day you "eat of it (the forbidden fruit), you will die the death." This sin manifested to Adam and Eve their own weakness, already present in the Garden of Eden, as the result of their *ontologically* prior and repressed *originative* sin, committed along with all the rest of us. The *original* sin in Eden has initiated the execution of the punishment of *originative* sin for all of us. It has included our generation in the world of space and time, that made it possible for us to wake up to our sinfulness and our need for a Savior.

Knowing

Knowing is, quintessentially, a personal activity by which we are related intentionally to the being and essence of everyone and everything. It is proper to all persons. Every person is *knowing*, even if unconsciously. Despite our present degree of consciousness, therefore, knowing is also vastly unconscious for us in the fallen world. The largely repressed origin of our unconscious knowing is our response in the moment of creation *ex nihilo*.

Starting from our present fixation on an implicit framework of space and time for everything, *we think that* conscious knowing in this world *initiates* the connection between knower and known, that is, between ourselves and the world we are knowing. But the connection or "intactness" is already there—having been buried by our initial ontological repression.

Knowing in the spatiotemporal world, then, is remedial. It is a knowing derivative of the primal knowing, done by our being as be-ing. It is the tip of the iceberg.

We cannot not know—however remotely and confusedly—all that is. To be is to know (finitely, for created persons) all that is—at least to some degree. God is known by everyone, whether consciously or unconsciously or partly both. So, too, is every being in creation, spiritual and temporal (past, present, and future). Unconscious, subconscious, and preconscious knowing are bases, out of which ordinary *conscious* knowing occurs.

Sensory knowing is also real, but peripheral, and not as such personal. By sensation *alone* (i.e. as in animals)—whether internal or external sense knowing—the *essence* of something can never be known. *Human* sense knowing, however, is essentially intellective.

We have been hardened perennially by the idea that there is nothing in the intellect that was not first in some manner in the senses. So, we are inclined to think that substantial knowing is a kind of "gap jumping." By the power of its "intentionality" (other-directedness) and by the light of an "agent intellect," the ordinary (potential) intellect is thought to initiate contact with the essences of people and things (called "objects" of knowledge) by 'jumping the gap' between knowing power and known realities.

Such a knowing, however, is to be found only in redemptive creation (*ex aliquo*). This knowing is itself founded on the gapless and super-dynamic radiation of knowledge coming from the nurturing originative knowing at the moment of creation *ex nihilo*. In that originative creation, we knew, *and still know, all that is*, by our *finite* powers of intellect and will, now so sorely self-damaged. The common practice that identifies our knowing as *solely within* our earthly predicament reinforces our originative repression and keeps us "locked out" of the depths of our be-ing and of the much fuller meaning for *who we are* even at present.

The empirical and quasi-empirical dimensions of intellection here and now must be supported by strictly non-empirical, but archetypally relevant dimensions. Wisdom is a loving kind of knowing and a knowing kind of love.

Conscious is the manner of knowing that we all rightly desire now. As experienced in the spatiotemporal world, conscious knowing is necessarily narrow and focused. It precludes much. Yet, before we know things consciously, we know them unconsciously, perhaps also subconsciously, definitely preconsciously, and above all, protoconsciously. Conscious knowledge and awareness of someone or something can come about in various ways (such as immediate intellection or intuition, instruction from another, recalling or memory, individual or collective probing and investigation, meditation, contemplation, and so forth).

Subconscious is the manner of knowing things that are just below the surface of ordinary consciousness. We are always knowing subconsciously particular things, many of which are semi-conscious, or at least partially conscious. Subconscious things often can be brought into consciousness. How to do ordinary tasks such as eating, washing dishes, playing tennis, playing the piano, and all manner of "automatic" activities constitute one major area of the subconscious.

Unconscious is the repressed manner of knowing persons, things, and meanings that are buried deeply away from conscious life. Much is rarely accessible to consciousness as formed in this world. But the whole of the unconscious plays a large part in influencing thought and behavior. It is meaningful to distinguish the emotional, that is, the psychic unconscious (recognized psychoanalytically) from the ontological unconscious, so prominent in this book.

We might even speak of the physical unconscious. It includes all human physiological and physical actions of which we are not overtly conscious. Together, the physical, the psychic, and the spiritual unconscious—including the "collective and archetypal unconscious"—form a virtually horizonless ocean of potential meaning.

Some have represented the unconscious as featuring levels. Included are the subconscious, along with various kinds of deeply buried meaning.

From the ontological standpoint of this book, we know *protoconsciously* everything that is. Such knowledge was "smashed and packed down" by the sin forming our *unconsciousness*. Therefore, when we consciously know something in this world, especially new meanings, we do not simply come to know it "out of the blue." Rather, we come to *know that we know* it finitely, and yet with much inadequacy.

Preconscious (non-Freudian) is the immediate manner of knowing persons and activities that are *spiritually unconscious*. Persons and activities that are critical to our sheer *being* are particularly known in this way. The preconscious area of reality occurs prior to the development of ordinary consciousness. It is most directly beingful in its bearing upon us. This ontological level of knowing—in this book, the spiritually unconscious—is quite closely associated with the protoconscious, our originative act of freedom in creation *ex nihilo*.

Protoconscious is the pure manner of knowing by which we originatively received our be-ing from God. It is our originative knowing of God, self, and all others at the non-durational, first moment of creation. This is the archetype of what we now know and call our consciousness: ordinary consciousness that is partial, functional, and privileged as redemptive.

Repression is the unconscious denial that we know some event, actuality, emotion, feeling, or value even as we *do know it unconsciously*. This mechanism of human knowing is an attempt to protect the knower from impulses, images, concepts, memories, meanings, and values that would likely cause anxiety and various disturbances. Repression is never good, but often inevitable.

The supreme instance of such "protection" is our immediate denial to ourselves of what we failed to do at the moment of being created out of nothing. This prime repression keeps us from recognizing our originative sin, the ultimate cause of *all* evil in our lives. It virtually requires blaming Adam, Eve, the serpent, and God for originating our predicament.

Psychoanalytic repression—repression of unwanted emotional and mental content—is better known at present and to be taken seriously; but it does not even get near to the root of our spiritual denial of originative sin. The latter is the supreme reason for all repression and suppression.

Suppression is the *conscious* attempt to be unaware of, or not to attend to, the multiplicity of events, actualities, emotions, feelings, or values that flood our everyday lives. Generally, it is a good and necessary endeavor that is ongoing and allows us to concentrate on one thing at a time. Often it is the explicitly deliberate attempt to block, however rapidly, awareness of something undesirable. This activity can be good or bad, depending on the issue at hand.

Suppression is a conscious activity, even if quick and minimally explicit. Repression, however, is always an unconscious activity.

Intellect

In the new view, intellect and will are co-dimensions of the *be-ing* that each created person *is*. They are the "know and love" powers of *be-ing*. To be, for a person, is to *know* and to *will*. A person cannot *be* without also knowing and willing *protoconsciously*—however well or poorly.

Intellect and will are more than simply faculties of reparative and recuperative action in the world of be-coming, as we first come to be aware of them. They *are* the created being as knowing and willing (loving or hating) originatively and forever.

Potential Intellect is the power to know *by which* we are in touch with, and called to become wedded to, the essence and being of everyone and everything good.

In our common earthly life, this power does the conceiving, judging, and reasoning. It operates in being determined ("stimulated") by the objects of knowledge. It is the ability to be-done-to by whatever it conceives. It is ecstatically fulfilled in heaven, and is an instrument of supreme self-torture in hell.

Agent intellect, in traditional thought from Aristotle onward, is a pure act of intelligibility-giving. It is characterized as a supreme light that renders what is potentially knowable by the potential intellect actually knowable. It is a supreme instrument of knowledge, without itself being a knowing power.

In the new view, however, agent intellect is the originative capacity to *know* (fully and directly)(a purely active power to know)—to be united with all persons, infinite and finite, in their being and essence. It is the only way *knowing* transpires in heaven.

Will

Potential Will is the power, in space and time, to love *by which* we affirm, and are called to unite with, the essence and the being of everyone and everything good. The objects of the will determine or "act upon" it in the holistic processes such as loving, desiring, delighting, being repelled, and the like. Thus will functions in the redemptive creation as a critical means of coming to what God has prepared for those who would love forever.

Agent Will is the power to love, to say *fully yes* to God, self, and others immediately and forever—right from the originative beginning. From "moment one" in creation, we did not fully exercise it. This power is now almost totally repressed.

In classical philosophy, the missing elements are curious concerning the agent (active) intellect and the agent (active) will. The agent intellect is portrayed as not knowing anything. And the notion of an agent will is virtually non-existent. But one cannot reasonably conceive of intellect without a corresponding will, and *vice versa*. That idea has been axiomatic in terms of the traditional understanding of potential intellect and potential will. Such can be no less true for active intellect and active will.

It is interesting to realize that the classical tradition recognizes, from the thought of Aristotle, the reality of an agent (purely active) *intellect*. But it fails to acknowledge it as *both* a light *and* a purely receptive knowing power for executing a pure act of knowing.

Nowhere, however, do we find acknowledgement of the truly agent (purely active) *will,* by which we committed our personal originative sin, but could have instead related perfectly with God forever.

At the heart of all knowing and loving, **agent intellect** is our purely active power of emphatically receiving ourselves and others, even as **agent will** is our purely active power of emphatically *gifting* to ourselves and others. In hell, **agent will** represses itself so severely that one can blame all adversity on God. In heaven, **agent will** is our central loving power, uniting us with God in utter bliss forever.

By their originatively defective activity, **agent intellect** and **agent will** are found in this world to have been largely passivized (contaminated). Yet every passive condition of intellection and of volition requires, as its base, a purely active agency, as gifted by God at the core of one's being. Only by **agent will**, for instance, can we love God with our "whole mind and heart." The slightest passivity prevents wholeness of activity.

Loving

Loving is willing the truest and best for self and *all* others, despite the cost. Not wanting or wishing, but *willing*. Our loving comes in degrees of intensity. At any given time, however, we love everyone, including God, with the same intensity. Often confused with liking, loving has nothing *essentially* to do with pleasure and pain. Love of enemies and of friends is the call to all that they may live well the be-ing with which they were originatively gifted.

At any given moment, we love everyone with the same *intensity*, but we know and love some persons with much greater *richness* than with others, based on our mutual experience, affection, and value sharing. If we were to consider whom we *love* least in this world: we can know that *that* is how *intensely* we love God, all others, and ourselves.

Affirmational love (see *loving*) is the central form of at least five kinds of love. Affirmation is the attitude of spontaneously delighting in another person and giving the other to himself or herself in an unqualified manner. The beloved feels loved and gifted as good unconditionally by the lover. Obviously, God is the supreme Gifter of being: of gifting to another (the created person) his or her whole being, without any "strings" attached.

Traditionally, *storge, eros, philia,* and *agape* are often cited. In general, they are forms either of giving others to self (such as *eros*) or of giving self to others (such as *agape*).

None of these, however, expresses the central meaning of love found in the *originative creation*. And when created persons come to realize *existentially* how they have been gifted by God, they are much better able to "pass it on" in attitude and in deed to their companions in being. God's act of creating was an *infinite willing* of each of us to *be*, to be this unique person, and to *be-with* God—literally giving us to ourselves to *be* forever.

Friendship is a relationship that is of genuine love (see above) in which the persons share some sense of equality and esteem, including affection, and an ever-increasing participation in common values. The depth of the friendship can be assessed by the degree to which the friends participate in the most fundamental, spiritual values of human life. We *love* our friends more richly than others, but not more intensely.

In brief, friendship is loving plus liking. It is opposite to "enemyship," that is, loving plus disliking.

Assorted Terms

Experience is the conscious participation in the world of space and time. It is essentially a *felt being-done-to*. It can be pleasant or unpleasant, happy or unhappy, by virtue of how one's consciousness is affected by the interaction with others and the movements of the self.

Experience is a bit like the wrapping or insulation on an electric wire. It can serve as a protection from what is really going on, what is going through the wire. Or it can be stripped away...by death. Experience is the conscious impact upon us of the world of passive potency.

But our activities or acts that the experience surrounds are independent of the "wrapping" or experience. We inveterately fail to identify the difference between acting and being acted upon while acting, even as we fail to identify the difference between being and existence. Ex-perience happens only in ex-istence and in our outsideness kind of agency. Every experience—including the mystical—"hides" an act or acting that is at least a little bit other than the experience itself, even as every existent—being that ex-ists—hides the act that is the be-ing of it all....However positive our experience is, it is basically passive (passive-reactive in the ontological sense).

There is no experience in heaven. No beatific *experience*. Just sheerly ecstatic, egoless participation in the Being of God and of one another—incomparably more joyful than any *experience*. The heart of acting and co-acting is passivity-free, existence-free, and experience-free. All is be-ing and lov-ing in consummate joy.

Experience provides opportunity for learning here in creation *ex aliquo*. But experience is not "the best teacher." It is not a teacher at all. The one who experiences teaches self or is taught *through* experience, not *by* it.

Perfection is a term that literally suggests the fulfillment of a process, a making (*per-ficere*, from *per-facere* to do or make through and through). Nevertheless, traditionally, it seems to be purged of any suggestion of process as when it is applied to God and angels. For the most part, it means *flawless, without blemish or defect*.

The scholastic philosophers and theologians made much of a distinction between what they called pure and mixed perfections. Pure perfections are those attributes such as intellect, knowledge, love, truth, *et al.* that do not necessarily suggest any passivity or "limitation." Mixed perfections are those qualities that necessarily are a mix of actuality and passive potency, such as colors, sounds, bodies, *et al.*

In the new view, these perspectives on perfection are included, but a new and critical emphasis is placed on the difference between perfection (flawlessness) that is *finite*, including the immediate *effects* of the divine Creator's action, and perfection that is *infinite* (God).

Created goodness, for instance, is not fulfilled in infinite Goodness, but in its own kind of *finite* gifted *perfection*.

We are fulfilled *by* God—and by our cooperative selves. But God is not (pantheistically) our fullness. This fullness is finitely perfect, not infinitely perfect. Infinite goodness is the only ultimate *cause* of our complete fulfillment, but not the fulfillment of our perfection itself.

Conception (human) is our individual entry into the cosmos. Prior to conception we were redeemable, but we would have been almost entirely dysfunctional. Conception is not the beginning of the person's *being*, but the *beginning* of the *becoming* (positive growth and awareness)—the person's coming back, within God's redeeming action, to a condition of originatively-intended *being*. Conception really *happens to* the person and initiates formal participation in the challenging spatiotemporal dimension of redemptive activity.

Death is the exit of a redeemed person from the opportunities of the awakening, alerting life in the cosmos. It is entry into everlasting destiny, through divine judgment—into heaven, hell, or final purgation for heaven. What is left in space and time are the *remains* of that person's cosmic participation. The corpse is not the body itself, but "exhaust" from the person's dynamic thrust through space and time.

The internal or spiritual body by which the earthly participation was specifically effected goes with the person and is not separated from the soul. What happens to be separated is the person's empirical (placenta-like) connectedness with life in cosmic matter.

The soul and the ontological body are reparative dimensions of the originative form (givity) and matter (receptivity) of the person. They could not really separate from each other, without loss of *essential ontological integrity*. In hell, they are "impossibly united" as essential parts and are inexorably at war with each other forever. In heaven, they are "radiantly harmonious" with each other forever.

Grace is the infinitely affirming Being of God as gifting us with the union of love and of perfect friendship. The grace of creation—being brought to be "out of nothing" in an unlimitedly unconditional way—is the supreme gift that we failed to receive *fully*. The grace involved in redemption and in salvation is the same open union of love offered to us in myriad ways.

Temptable is the condition of human persons who said *maybe* to the gift of being originatively. God's creation *ex nihilo* could only be infinitely perfect, yielding finitely perfect effects. These created persons were not temptable as gifted, but *as received.* "God's best" needs no test. But they immediately rendered themselves imperfect. They were thereby in need of testing or revealing—to themselves and to others—how reliable they could be.

Adam and Eve and their historic children, with two notable exceptions, were to be tested by being tempted throughout their lives, however long or short these might be. Death might bring on some of the most dreadful temptations for many. Temptability itself indicates the need of salvation and provides a necessary sign of anyone who has committed an originative sin.

Reincarnation is impossible. The intrinsic integrity of body and soul as the remedial dimensions of the *originative* matter (receptivity) and form (givity) of human being make such theory absurd. The form and matter of the person are absolutely *essential, correlative parts* of the very *essence* of human personhood.

Reincarnation is an attempt to make intelligible the 'law of karma' that is supposed to need many bodies for mediation over lengthy periods of soul activity, picking up and discarding bodies. Personal identity is egregiously compromised. And body is demeaned, along with the soul.

Likewise, in the Western world, the traditional theory of hylomorphism (matter-and-form) has not succeeded in telling adequately of the integrity of human beings within their essence. If God's absolute act of creating perfect essences *ex nihilo* is adequately recognized, the soul cannot be *separated* from the body, in the way that classical theology has conceived it, any more than the form can be separate from the matter. The activity essential to persons receiving redemption—who are *becoming,* that is, being *created ex aliquo*—requires genuine self-identity at every point in the process, including especially the period between death and the final resurrection.

Human Life and Sexuality Series

Along with others, this book by Mary Rosera Joyce:

The Future of Adam and Eve: Finding the Lost Gift

(LifeCom, 2009) 267 pages

Adam's Puritan-Playboy America; True Sexual Freedom; Friendship; Sexual Likeness to God; True Feminism; Sexuality and the Trinity; the Meaning of Personhood; the Origin of Evil; *et al.*

Two Creations Series

In addition to the book, *God Said, We Said*, there are others by R. E. Joyce:

Affirming Our Freedom in God:
The Untold Story of Creation

(LifeCom, 2001) 100 pages.

The Cry of Why, beneath the Holocaust; Are We Hiding Something? God Freely Creates Our Freedom to Create, *et al.*

Facing the Dark Side of Genesis:
A New Understanding of Ourselves

(LifeCom, 2008) 84 pages.

The Genesis Gap; Originative Sin; Theology of the Person's Being; Two Creations: Originative and Redemptive; Consequences for a Life of Faith, *et al.*

A Perfect Creation:
The Light behind the Dark Side of Genesis

(LifeCom, 2008) 170 pages.

From Cosmess to Cosmos; The Missing Infinity of God; God's Intimate Act of Creation; The Meaning of Evil and Its Cause, *et al.*

The following two books form a trilogy with the present one and are part of the comprehensive volume: *When God Said Be, We Said Maybe: An Inside Story of the Creation, the Crash, and the Recovery of Being* (LifeCom 2011)

God Says, We Say: The Interpersonal Act of Redemption (LifeCom 2010)

God Will Say, We Will Say: The Interpersonal Act of Salvation (LC 2010)

LifeCom   **Box 1832, St. Cloud, MN 56302**
www.Lifemeaning.com

www.ingramcontent.com/pod-product-compliance
Lightning Source LLC
Chambersburg PA
CBHW022023090426
42739CB00006BA/255